Charles Stedman Newhall

The Shrubs of Northeastern America

Charles Stedman Newhall

The Shrubs of Northeastern America

ISBN/EAN: 9783337219543

Printed in Europe, USA, Canada, Australia, Japan

Cover: Foto ©ninafisch / pixelio.de

More available books at **www.hansebooks.com**

THE SHRUBS

OF

NORTHEASTERN AMERICA

BY

CHARLES S. NEWHALL

AUTHOR OF "THE TREES OF NORTHEASTERN AMERICA," ETC.

G. P. PUTNAM'S SONS
NEW YORK   LONDON
27 WEST TWENTY-THIRD ST.   24 BEDFORD ST., STRAND
The Knickerbocker Press
1897

COPYRIGHT, 1891
BY
CHARLES S. NEWHALL

Electrotyped, Printed, and Bound by
The Knickerbocker Press, New York
G. P. Putnam's Sons

THE SHRUBS.

'T is true, among the brotherhood
Of regal trees that hold their place
Like sceptred kings, you have no rank,
Dear children of the humbler race.

Instead you ever seem to stand
In mute appeal for love and care,
With offered gifts of grace and bloom,
In lowly places everywhere.

But, children of the humbler race,
'T is therefor that we give you praise.
You give your souls (your flowers), and we
Our love, through all the changing days.

CONTENTS.

	PAGE
LIST OF ILLUSTRATIONS	vii
PREFACE	xi
LIST OF FAMILIES AND OF GENERA	13
DIRECTIONS, SIGNS USED, ETC.	17
GUIDE TO THE SHRUBS (by Flower. Natural Arrangement.)	19
GUIDE TO THE SHRUBS (by Leaf.)	25
GUIDE TO THE SHRUBS (by Fruit.)	29
DESCRIPTION OF SHRUBS (with Illustrations.)	34–233
Angiospérmæ, mostly with Distinct Petals	34–129
" " " United "	130–192
" with Petals Lacking	194–228
Gymnospérmæ	230–233
SHRUBS NOT ELSEWHERE NAMED	233
EXPLANATION OF TERMS	236
GLOSSARY	240
LIST OF SHRUBS WORTHY OF CULTIVATION	241
INDEX TO THE SHRUBS	243

ILLUSTRATIONS.

	PAGE
Figure 1.—SHRUB YELLOW-ROOT	35
Figure 2.—SWEET-BAY	37
Figure 3.—PAPAW	39
Figure 4.—BARBERRY	41
Figure 5.—HUDSONIA	41
Figure 6.—ST.-PETER'S-WORT	43
Figure 7.—SHRUBBY ST.-JOHN'S-WORT	43
Figure 8.—PRICKLY ASH	49
Figure 9.—HOP TREE	51
Figure 10.—ILEX	53
Figure 11.—WINTERBERRY	53
Figure 12.—INKBERRY	55
Figure 13.—MOUNTAIN HOLLY	57
Figure 14.—BURNING-BUSH	59
Figure 15.—STRAWBERRY-BUSH	59
Figure 16.—LANCE-LEAVED BUCKTHORN	63
Figure 17.—ALDER-LEAVED BUCKTHORN	63
Figure 18.—NARROW-LEAVED CEANOTHUS	65
Figure 19.—NEW JERSEY TEA	65
Figure 20.—MOUNTAIN MAPLE	67
Figure 21.—BLADDER-NUT	69
Figure 22.—SMOOTH SUMACH	71
Figure 23.—DWARF SUMACH	71
Figure 24.—POISON SUMACH	75

	PAGE
Figure 25.—Poison Ivy	77
Figure 26.—Sweet Sumach	77
Figure 27.—False Indigo	79
Figure 28.—Wild Plum	83
Figure 29.—Beach Plum	83
Figure 30.—Sloe [P. spinosa]	85
Figure 31.—Choke-Cherry	85
Figure 32.—Meadow-Sweet	87
Figure 33.—Birch-Leaved Spiræa	87
Figure 34.—Hardhack	89
Figure 35.—Nine-Bark	89
Figure 36.—Purple-Flowering Raspberry	91
Figure 37.—Red Raspberry	93
Figure 38.—Blackcap	95
Figure 39.—Bland Rose	99
Figure 40.—Chokeberry	101
Figure 41.—Dogberry	101
Figure 42.—White Thorn	105
Figure 43.—Black Thorn	105
Figure 44.—Cockspur Thorn	107
Figure 45.—Dwarf Thorn	107
Figure 46.—June-Berry	109
Figure 47.—Sweet-Scented Shrub	109
Figure 48.—Wild Hydrángea	113
Figure 49.—Itea	115
Figure 50.—Prickly Gooseberry	115
Figure 51.—Swamp Gooseberry	117
Figure 52.—Wild Red Currant	117
Figure 53.—Witch-Hazel	119
Figure 54.—Angelica Tree	123
Figure 55.—Round-Leaved Cornel	125
Figure 56.—Common Elder	131
Figure 57.—Hobble-Bush	135
Figure 58.—Bush Cranberry	137
Figure 59.—Maple-Leaved Arrow-wood	139

Illustrations

Figure 60.—ARROW-WOOD.
Figure 61.—DOWNY ARROW-WOOD.
Figure 62.—WITHE-ROD (V. NÙDUM)
Figure 63.—BLACK HAW.
Figure 64.—SNOWBERRY.
Figure 65.—INDIAN CURRANT.
Figure 66.—FLY-HONEYSUCKLE.
Figure 67.—BUSH HONEYSUCKLE.
Figure 68.—BUTTON-BUSH.
Figure 69.—GROUNDSEL TREE.
Figure 70.—COMMON BLACK HUCKLEBERRY.
Figure 71.—DANGLEBERRY.
Figure 72.—SQUAW HUCKLEBERRY.
Figure 73.—COMMON LOW BLUEBERRY.
Figure 74.—COMMON HIGH BLUEBERRY.
Figure 75.—MARSH ANDRÓMEDA.
Figure 76.—STAGGER-BUSH.
Figure 77.—PRIVET ANDRÓMEDA.
Figure 78.—LEUCÓTHOË.
Figure 79.—LEATHER-LEAF.
Figure 80.—MOUNTAIN LAUREL.
Figure 81.—SHEEP LAUREL.
Figure 82.—CLAMMY AZALEA.
Figure 83.—PURPLE AZALEA.
Figure 84.—GREAT LAUREL.
Figure 85.—RHODÓRA.
Figure 86.—LABRADOR TEA.
Figure 87.—SWEET PEPPER-BUSH.
Figure 88.—FRINGE-TREE.
Figure 89.—SPICE-BUSH.
Figure 90.—LEATHERWOOD.
Figure 91.—SHEPHERDIA.
Figure 92.—AMERICAN MISTLETOE.
Figure 93.—OIL-NUT.
Figure 94.—BAYBERRY.

Illustrations

	PAGE
Figure 95.—Sweet-Gale	203
Figure 96.—Sweet-Fern	203
Figure 97.—Low Birch	207
Figure 98.—Smooth Alder	211
Figure 99.—Hazel-nut	213
Figure 100.—Beaked Hazel-nut	213
Figure 101.—Hornbeam	215
Figure 102.—Dwarf Chestnut Oak	217
Figure 103.—Bear Oak	217
Figure 104.—Dwarf Chestnut	219
Figure 105.—Long-Leaved Willow	221
Figure 106.—Prairie Willow	221
Figure 107.—Dwarf Gray Willow	221
Figure 108.—Silky Willow	221
Figure 109.—Long-Stalked Green Osier	221
Figure 110.—Sage Willow	225
Figure 111.—Heart-Leaved Willow	225
Figure 112.—Pear-Leaved Willow	225
Figure 113.—Salix Myrtillòides	225
Figure 114.—Broom Crow-Berry	227
Figure 115.—Common Juniper	231
Figure 116.—American Yew	231

PREFACE.

I.

"C——, now that you have finished your book about the trees, I wish you would make another, this time about our native shrubs."

"Why?"

"Partly because I want to know the shrubs as I have learned to know the trees, and partly for another reason. You remember the little place I have in the country?"

"Yes, a pretty place that could be made prettier."

"Well, I had thought of finding a gardener and telling him to stock it as he chose, but I have a fancy that the result would be better every way if I and the children were to search the woods and so stock it for ourselves."

"And you want me to help you in your miniature landscape gardening."

"I want you to help me to know all our shrubs, and among them to know the best for the garden and the lawn. Will you?"

"Yes."

II.

In the introduction to *The Trees of Northeastern America*, I referred to the interest which one who visits the woods often takes in personal fellowship with the individual trees. He is not satisfied to pass through a forest or a field as one might walk the streets of a crowded city—unacquainted. His mood is friendly; therefore he is pleased when by any chance he can know the trees as friends, in their home life, intimately and by name.

One has a similar feeling toward the humbler company of the shrubs.

As I undertook the pleasant work of introduction between the many who have no technical botanical knowledge and my friend the trees, now I do the same for them and my friends the shrubs.

III.

The shrubs described in the following pages are those which are found native in Canada and the United States east of the Mississippi River and north of the latitude of Southern Pennsylvania. With these are described the more important of the introduced and naturalized species.

The woody vines of the section are not included. They are reserved for another volume.

I am glad to acknowledge my obligations to Dr. Thomas Morong, and again to Professor N. L. Britton of Columbia College. Professor Britton has very kindly revised the nomenclature of the shrubs. For the localities I have chiefly followed Gray and Wood. I am indebted also to the works of Torrey, Emerson, Millspaugh, Meehan, and others.

LIST OF FAMILIES AND OF GENERA.

Family 1. RANUNCULÀCEÆ (Crowfoot Fam.) — Genus Xanthorhiza (Shrub Yellow-root).

Family 2. MAGNOLIÀCEÆ (Magnolia Fam.) — Genus Magnòlia (Magnolia).

Family 3. ANONÀCEÆ (Papaw Fam.) — Genus Asimina (Papaw).

Family 4. BERBERIDÀCEÆ (Barberry Fam.) — Genus Bérberis (Barberry).

Family 5. CISTÀCEÆ (Rock-rose Fam.) — Genus Hudsònia (Hudsonia).

Family 6. HYPERICÀCEÆ (St.-John's-wort Fam.) — Genus Aścyrum (St.-Peter's-wort).
Genus Hypéricum (St.-John's-wort).

Family 7. RUTÀCEÆ (Rue Fam.) — Genus Xanthóxylum (Prickly Ash).
Genus Ptélea (Shrubby Trefoil).

Family 8. ILICÍNEÆ (Holly Fam.) — Genus Ílex (Holly, etc.).
Genus Nemopánthes (Mt. Holly).

Family 9. CELASTRÀCEÆ (Staff-tree Fam.) — Genus Euónymus (Burning-Bush.)

Family 10. RHAMNÀCEÆ (Buckthorn Fam.) — Genus Rhamnus (Buckthorns).
Genus Ceanòthus (New Jersey Tea, etc.).

Family 11. SAPINDÀCEÆ — Genus Acer (Maple).
Genus Staphylèa (Bladdernut).

Family 12. ANACARDIÀCEÆ (Sumach Fam.) — Genus Rhus (Sumachs).

Family 13. LEGUMINÒSÆ (Pulse Fam.) — Genus Amórpha (False Indigo).

Family 14. ROSÀCEÆ (Rose Fam.) Genus Prunus (Plum, Cherry).
Genus Spirǽa (Meadow-sweet, etc.).
Genus Physocárpus (Nine-bark).
Genus Rùbus (Blackberry, etc.).
Genus Ròsa (Rose).
Genus Pỳrus (Chokeberry, etc.).
Genus Cratǽgus (Thorn, Haw).
Genus Amelánchior (June-berry).

Family 15. CALYCANTHÀCEÆ (Caly-canthus Fam.) Genus Calycánthus (Sweet-scented Shrub).

Family 16. SAXIFRAGÀCEÆ (Saxifrage Fam.) Genus Hydrángea.
Genus Ítea.
Genus Ribes (Currant, etc.).

Family 17. HAMAMELÍDEÆ (Witch Hazel Fam.) Genus Hamámelis (Witch Hazel).

Family 18. ARALIÀCEÆ (Ginseng Fam.) Genus Arália (Angelica Tree).

Family 19. CORNÀCEÆ (Dogwood Fam.) Genus Cornus (Dogwoods or Cornels).

Family 20. CAPRIFOLIÀCEÆ (Honey-suckle Fam.) Genus Sambùcus (Elders).
Genus Vibúrnum (Arrow-woods, etc.).
Genus Symphoricárpos (Snowberry, etc.).
Genus Lonicèra (Fly-Honey-suckles).
Genus Diervílla (Bush Honeysuckle).

Family 21. RUBIÀCEÆ (Madder Fam.) Genus Cephalánthus (But-ton-bush).

Family 22. COMPÓSITÆ (Composite Fam.) Genus Báccharis (Groundsel Tree).
Genus Íva, L. (Marsh Elder).

Family 23. ERICÀCEÆ (Heath Fam.) Genus Gaylussàcia (Huckle-berry).

List of Families and of Genera

Family 23. ERICÀCEÆ (Heath Fam.)—
Continued.
    Genus Vaccínium (Blueberry, etc.).
    Genus Andrómeda.
    Genus Leucóthoë.
    Genus Cassándra.
    Genus Kálmia (Laurels, etc.).
    Genus Menziésia.
    Genus Rhododéndron (Azaleas, etc.).
    Genus Ledum (Labrador Tea).
    Genus Clethra (Sweet Pepper-bush).

Family 24. OLEÀCEÆ (Olive Fam.)
    Genus Chionánthus (Fringe Tree).
    Genus Ligústrum (Privet).

Family 25. LAURÀCEÆ (Laurel Fam.)
    Genus Líndera (Spice-bush).

Family 26. THYMELÀCEÆ (Daphne Fam.)
    Genus Dírca (Leatherwood).
    Genus Dáphne (Mezéreum).

Family 27. ELÆAGNÀCEÆ (Oleaster Fam.)
    Genus Shephérdia.

Family 28. LORANTHÀCEÆ (Mistletoe Fam.)
    Genus Phoradéndron (Am. Mistletoe).

Family 29. SANTALÀCEÆ (Sandalwood Fam.)
    Genus Pyrulària (Oil-nut).

Family 30. MYRICÀCEÆ (Sweet-Gale Fam.)
    Genus Myrìca (Bayberry, etc.).

Family 31. CUPULÍFERÆ (Oak, etc., Fam.)
    Genus Bétula (Birches).
    Genus Álnus (Alders).
    Genus Córylus (Hazel-nuts).
    Genus Carpìnus (Hornbeam).
    Genus Quércus (Oaks).
    Genus Castànea (Dwarf Chestnut).

Family 32. SALICÀCEÆ (Willow Fam.)
    Genus Sàlix (Willows).

Family 33. EMPETRÀCEÆ (Crow-berry Fam.)
    Genus Corèma (Broom Crow-berry).
    Genus Émpetrum (Black Crow-berry).

Family 34. CONÍFERÆ (Pine Fam.)
    Genus Juníperus (Juniper).
    Genus Taxus (Am. Yew).

DIRECTIONS.

Note 1. The place of any given specimen can be readily found by help of one or more of the three "Guides" given on pages 1 to 10.

The first Guide is arranged for use with the flowers; the second, with the leaves; the third, with the fruit. Which of the three can be used to the best advantage will depend upon the time of year.

The descriptions are scientific but not technical.

Note 2. In describing a species, the general items that have been given under the genus or the family to which the species belongs are not usually repeated.

Note 3. In using the Leaf Guide and the leaf illustrations it should be remembered that leaves from vigorous young sprouts are not usually the best specimens. It is seldom that two leaves, even upon the same mature plant, exactly agree, but they follow the type, while often the younger growth varies from it.

Note 4. Those species are considered shrubs (in distinction from trees) which, as the rule, do not spring from the ground with a single branching trunk.

Note 5. Signs used: A grave accent (ˋ) over a vowel indicates that it is accented and long. An acute accent (ˊ) over a vowel indicates that it is accented and short.

Names enclosed in brackets indicate that the shrub is not native.

GUIDE I.

FLOWERS.

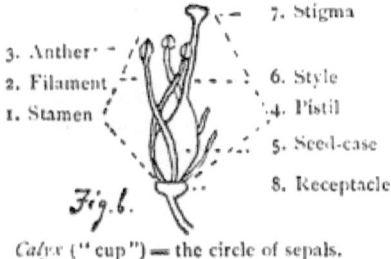

Corolla ("crown") = the circle of petals.

Calyx ("cup") = the circle of sepals.

For further explanation of terms see Glossary, page 240.

CLASS FIRST.—Young seeds enclosed in a seed-case (Angiospérmæ), including all shrubs excepting those of the Pine Family.

DIVISION I. Sepals and petals both present, the latter not united into one piece (Polypetalous).
  A. Stamens numerous, at least more than ten.
    1. Sepals attached below the seed-case or cases.
      (*a*) Seed-cases numerous, but clinging together in a solid mass on a lengthened receptacle. Blossoms one and one-half inches or more across. Petals and sepals colored alike. Sweet-Bay in Magnolia Fam. No. 2 (Magnoliàceæ), page 36.
      (*a*) Seed-cases numerous, separate, concealed in an urn-shaped or cup-shaped receptacle.
        (*b*) Leaves opposite, entire. Calycanthus Fam. No. 15 (Calycanthàceæ) page 110.

- (*b*) Leaves alternate, toothed. The Rose in Rose Fam. No. 14 (Rosàceæ), page 96.
- (*a*) Seed-cases more than one, separate, not enclosed in the receptacle. Rose Fam. (in part) No. 14 (Rosàceæ), page 80, *seq.*
- (*a*) Pistil, one.
  - (*b*) Flowers yellowish; leaves opposite, edge entire, dotted (under a lens). St.-John's-wort Fam. No. 6 (Hypericàceæ), page 44.
  - (*b*) Flowers white or pinkish; leaves alternate, toothed. Plums and Cherries in Rose Fam. No. 14 (Rosàceæ), pages 80–84.
  - (*b*) Flowers bright-yellow, small, lasting only a day; leaves crowded, scale-like or awl-shaped, downy. Hudsonia in Rock-Rose Fam. No. 5 (Cistàceæ), page 42.
2. Sepals attached to the seed-case.
  - (*a*) Seed-case ten-celled, with one seed in each cell. Shadbush in Rose Fam. No. 14 (Rosàceæ), page 108.
  - (*a*) Seed-case two- to five-celled. Chokeberry and Haw in Rose Fam. No. 14 (Rosàceæ), pages 100–104.

B. Stamens of the same number as the petals, and opposite to them.
  - (*a*) Flowers yellow; seed-case with one cell. Barberry Fam. No. 4 (Berberidàceæ) page 38.
  - (*a*) Flowers greenish; seed-case with two to four cells. Buckthorn Fam. No. 10 (Rhamnàceæ), page 61.

C. Stamens, not more than twice as many as the petals; when of just the number, alternate with them.
  1. Sepals attached below the seed-case or cases.
    - (*a*) Seed-cases, two or more, separate.
      - (*b*) Stamens attached to the receptacle.
        - (*c*) Flowers greenish or whitish. Rue Fam. No. 7 (Rutàceæ), page 47.
        - (*c*) Flowers brownish-purple. Crowfoot Fam. No. 1 (Ranunculàceæ), page 34.
      - (*b*) Stamens attached to the sepals. Spiræa in Rose Fam. No. 14 (Rosàceæ), page 86.
    - (*a*) Seed-case, one.
      - (*b*) Seed-case with one cell.
        - (*c*) Petal, only one; flowers violet or purple. False Indigo in Pulse Fam. No. 13 (Leguminòsæ), page 78.

Flowers

- (*c*) Petals, five and equal; flowers greenish-white or yellowish; seed, one. Sumach Fam. No. 12 (Anacardiàceæ), page 70.
- (*c*) Petals, five and equal, but lasting only for a day; flowers light-yellow; seeds, several. Hudsonia in Rock-Rose Fam. No. 5 (Cistàceæ), page 42.
- (*c*) Petals, five and equal; flowers white; seeds, several. Ítea in Saxifrage Fam. No. 16 (Saxifragàceæ), page 112.
- (*b*) Seed-case with two to several cells.
  - (*c*) Flowers irregular. Rhododendron in Heath Fam. No. 23 (Ericàceæ), page 178.
  - (*c*) Flowers regular.
    - (*d*) Stamens, two (early, three or four); petals, four, barely united at base. Fringe Tree in Olive Fam. No. 24 (Oleàceæ), page 190.
    - (*d*) Stamens more numerous than the petals. Maple in Soapberry Fam. No. 11 (Sapindàceæ), page 66.
    - (*d*) Stamens just as many or twice as many as the petals.
      - (*e*) Seeds, only one or two in each cell.
        - (*f*) Leaves compound, of three leaflets. Hop Tree in Rue Fam. No. 7 (Rutàceæ), page 50.
        - (*f*) Leaves simple.
          - (*g*) Sepals not minute. Euónymus in Staff-Tree Fam. No. 9 (Celastràceæ), page 58.
          - (*g*) Sepals minute. Holly Fam. No. 8 (Ilicíneæ), page 50.
      - (*e*) Seeds, several or many in each cell.
        - (*f*) Leaves compound and opposite. Bladder-Nut in Soapberry Fam. No. 11 (Sapindàceæ), page 68.
        - (*f*) Leaves simple, alternate.
          - (*g*) Edge entire. Lèdum in Heath Fam. No. 23 (Ericàceæ), page 186.
          - (*g*) Edge-toothed. Cléthra in Heath Fam. No. 23 (Ericàceæ), page 188.

2. Sepals attached to the seed-case.
   - (*a*) Young seeds, more than one in each cell.
     - (*b*) Seed-case with one cell; leaves alternate. Currant and Gooseberry in Saxifrage Fam. No. 16 (Saxifragàceæ), page 114.

- (*b*) Seed-case with two to several cells; leaves opposite.
  - (*c*) Petals rounded; stamens, four to five, very short. Spindle-Tree in Staff-Tree Fam. No. 9 (Celastràceæ), page 58.
  - (*c*) Petals egg-shape; stamens, eight to ten, slender. Hydrángea in Saxifrage Fam. No. 16 (Saxifragàceæ), page 111.
- (*a*) Young seeds, only one in each cell.
  - (*b*) Stamens, ten or five; leaves simple. Cratægus in Rose Fam. No. 14 (Rosàceæ), page 103.
  - (*b*) Stamens, four; flowers dark-purple. Spindle-Tree in Staff-Tree Fam. No. 9 (Celastràceæ), page 58.
  - (*b*) Perfect stamens, four; flowers yellow. Witch-Hazel Fam. No. 17 (Hamamelídeæ), page 118.
  - (*b*) Stamens, four; flowers white. Dogwood Fam. No. 19 (Cornàceæ), page 124.
  - (*b*) Stamens, five; leaves compound. Angelica Tree in Ginseng Fam. No. 18 (Araliàceæ), page 122.

DIVISION II. Sepals and petals both present; the latter more or less united into one piece (Gamopetalous).

A. Stamens more numerous than the united petals. Heath Fam. No. 23 (Ericàceæ), page 155.

B. Stamens of the same number as the united petals, and alternate with them, or fewer.
  1. Sepals attached to the seed-case.
     - (*a*) Flowers in few- to many-blossomed heads, tubular, some with stamens only, others with pistils only; leaves alternate, or, in Iva, the lower ones opposite. Iva and Groundsel Tree in Composite Fam. No. 22 (Compósitæ), page 154.
     - (*a*) Flowers not crowded in round balls; leaves opposite. Honeysuckle Fam. No. 20 (Caprifoliàceæ), page 130.
     - (*a*) Flowers crowded in round balls; leaves opposite. Buttonbush in Madder Fam. No. 21 (Rubiàceæ), page 152.
  2. Sepals not attached to the seed-case.
     - (*a*) Corolla somewhat irregular. Rhododendron in Heath Fam. No. 23 (Ericàceæ), page 178.
     - (*a*) Corolla regular.
       - (*b*) Stamens of the same number as the united petals.
         - (*c*) Stamens free from the petals but inserted with them; style one. Heath Fam. No. 23 (Ericàceæ), page 155.

Flowers

- (c) Stamens attached to the base of the barely united petals; style none or very short. Holly Fam. No. 8 (Ilicineæ), page 50.
- (b) Stamens fewer than the four barely united, strap-like petals (rarely of the same number). Fringe Tree in Olive Fam. No. 24 (Oleàceæ), page 190.

DIVISION III. Petals (and sometimes sepals) wanting (apetalous).

A. Flowers not in slender, drooping, and scaly clusters, nor in scaly heads.
- (a) Seed-cases three to five and separate. Prickly Ash in Rue Fam. No. 7 (Rutàceæ), page 47.
- (a) Seed-case one.
  - (b) Sepals attached to the seed-case.
    - (c) Parasitic on the branches of trees. Mistletoe Fam. No. 28 (Loranthàceæ), page 199.
    - (c) Not parasitic; flowers small, greenish, in short spikes. Oil-Nut in Sandalwood Fam. No. 29 (Santalàceæ), page 200.
  - (b) Sepals not attached to the seed-case, but surrounding it; flowers small yellowish; leaves scurfy. Shephérdia in Oleaster Fam. No. 27 (Elæagnàceæ), page 198.
  - (b) Sepals sometimes wanting; when present plainly not attached to the seed-case.
    - (c) Young seeds, two in each cell. Maple in Soapberry Fam. No. 11 (Sapindàceæ), page 66.
    - (c) Young seeds, one in each cell.
      - (d) Cells of seed-case three to nine; leaves narrow, heath-like. Crow-Berry Fam. No. 33 (Empetràceæ), page 226.
      - (d) Cells of seed-case three; leaves broad. Buckthorn Fam. No. 10 (Rhamnàceæ), page 61.
      - (d) Cells of seed-case one.
        - (e) Flowers light-yellow; three or four in a simple cluster. Leatherwood in Daphne Fam. No. 26 (Thymelàceæ), page 196.
        - (e) Flowers light-yellow, many in a compound cluster. Spice-bush in Laurel Fam. No. 25 (Lauràceæ), page 194.

B. Flowers in slender, drooping, and scaly clusters, or in scaly heads, and of two sorts, with stamens only (staminate), and with pistils only (pistillate).

(*a*) Seed-cases two- to seven-celled, with one or two young seeds in each cell; in fruit one-celled and one-seeded; staminate flowers mostly in slender, drooping, and scaly clusters.   Oak Fam. No. 31 (Cupuliferæ) page 206.
(*a*) Seed-case one-celled with many young seeds; in fruit one-celled and many-seeded; staminate and pistillate flowers mostly in lengthened and scaly clusters. Willow Fam. No. 32 (Salicàceæ), page 220.
(*a*) Seed-case one-celled, with one young seed; staminate and pistillate flowers mostly in scaly heads; leaves fragrant when crushed. Sweet-Gale Fam. No. 30 (Myricàceæ) page 202.

CLASS SECOND.—Young seeds not enclosed in seed-cases; (Gymnospérmæ); leaves needle-shaped or line-like. Juniper and Yew in Pine Fam. No. 34 (Coníferæ) pages 230, 232.

GUIDE II.

LEAVES.

A. Leaves simple.*
  I. Alternate.
    (*a*) Edge entire. Go to 1.
    (*a*) " toothed. Go to 2.
    (*a*) " lobed.
      (*b*) Lobes entire. Go to 3.
      (*b*) " toothed. Go to 4.
  II. Opposite.
    (*a*) Edge entire. Go to 5.
    (*a*) " toothed. Go to 6.
    (*a*) " lobed.
      (*b*) Lobes entire. Go to 7.
      (*b*) " toothed. Go to 8.
  III. Indeterminate (because of smallness or closeness). Go to 9.
B. Leaves compound.
  I. Feather-shaped.
    (*a*) Alternate.
      (*b*) Edge of leaflets entire. Go to 10.
      (*b*) " " toothed. Go to 11.
    (*a*) Opposite.
      (*b*) Edge of leaflets entire. Go to 12.
      (*b*) " " toothed. Go to 13.
  II. Hand-shaped. Go to 14.

* The leaflets of a compound leaf can be distinguished from a simple leaf by the absence of leaf-buds from the base of their stems.

GUIDE II.

LEAVES—*Continued.*

NOTE.—Names in *italics* are also given elsewhere under the more frequent form.

1

Sweet-Bay, page 36.
Papaw, page 38.
Mountain Holly, page 56.
Cornel, alternate leaves, page 127.
Groundsel Tree, page 154.
Genus Gaylussàcia (Huckleberries and Dangleberries), excepting Box Huckleberry, page 204.
Genus Vaccinium (Blueberries and Bilberries), excepting Dwarf Blueberry and some Bilberries, page 162.
Genus Andrómeda, page 166.
Leather-leaf, page 171.
Mountain Laurel, page 174.
Genus Rhododéndron (Azaleas, etc.), excepting Sweet Pepper-bush, page 182.
Leatherwood, page 196.
Daphne, page 198.
Shepherdia, page 198.
Buffalo-Nut, page 200.
Bayberry, page 202.
Willows in part, page 220.

2

Barberry (thorny), page 38.
Ilex montícola, G., page 52.
Winterberry, page 52.
Inkberry (toothed toward apex), page 54.

Mt. Holly, page 56.
Buckthorns, page 61.
New Jersey Tea (strongly three-ribbed), page 64
Ceanòthus, narrow-leaved (strongly three-ribbed), page 64.
Genus Prùnus (Plum, Cherry, etc.), page 81.
Genus Spirǽa (Spirǽas), page 86.
Genus Pỳrus (Chokeberry, etc.), page 100.
Genus Cratǽgus in part (Thorns), page 104.
Genus Amelánchier (Shad-bush), page 108.
Itea, page 112.
Witch-Hazel (teeth large and rounded), page 118.
Groundsel Tree (teeth large and remote), page 154.
Dwarf Huckleberry, page 158.
Box Huckleberry, page 159.
Dwarf Blueberry and var., page 162.
Low Blueberry, page 163.
Some Bilberries, page 164.
Privet Andrómeda, page 169.
Leucòthoë, page 169.
Leather-Leaf, page 171.
Sweet Pepper-Bush, page 188.
Spice-Bush, page 194.
Genus Myrìca (Sweet Fern, etc., foliage fragrant), page 205.

Family Cupulíferæ (Birch, Alder, Hazel-nut, Hornbeam, Oak, Chestnut), except Bear Oak, page 206.
Willows in part, page 220.

3
Oak, Bear, page 218.

4
Nine-bark, page 88.
Raspberry, Flowering, page 90.
Genus Cratægus (in part Thorns), page 104.
Genus Ribes (Gooseberries), page 114.

5
St.-John's-worts (leaves minutely dotted) page 44.
Genus Córnus (Cornels) excepting C. alternifòlia, page 126.
Vibúrnum nùdum, page 140.
" cassinòides, page 142.
Snowberry, page 144.
Wolfberry, page 144.
Indian Currant, page 146.
Genus Lonicèra (Honeysuckles), page 148
Button-Bush, page 152.
Genus Kàlmia (Laurels), page 174.
Fringe-Tree, page 190.
Privet, page 190.
Mistletoe, page 199.
Juniper (in threes, needle-like), page 230

6
Burning-Bush, page 58.
Strawberry-Bush, page 60.

Sweet-scented Shrub, page 110.
Hydrángea, page 111.
Hobble-Bush, page 134.
Genus Vibúrnum, in part (Downy Vibúrnum, Arrow-wood, Soft Vibúrnum, Black Haw, *V. nùdum, V. cassinòides*), page 140.
Bush Honeysuckle, page 150.
Marsh Elder, page 154.

7
Sweet Fern, page 205.

8
Mt. Maple, page 66.
Genus Vibúrnum in part (Cranberry Tree, Dockmackie, Few-flowered Viburnum), page 134.

9
Hudsonias, page 42.
Broom Crow-Berry, page 226.
Black Crow-Berry, page 228.
Juniper, page 230.
Yew, American, page 232.

10
Prickly Ash, page 47.
Trefoil Shrubby, page 50.
Ivy, Poison, page 76.
Indigo, False, page 78.
Lead Plant, page 78.

11
Shrub Yellow-Root, page 34.
Prickly Ash, page 47.
Trefoil Shrubby, page 50.
Sumachs, page 70.
Ivy Poison, page 76.

12

Genus Rùbus (Raspberries, Blackberries, etc.), except Flowering Raspberry, page 92.
Genus Ròsa (Rose), page 98.
Angelica Tree, page 122.

13

Bladder-Nut (three leaflets), page 68.
Elders, page 130.

14

GUIDE III.

FRUIT.

CLASS I.—Fruit releasing the ripened seed by decaying:

A. Fleshy or pulpy, with one or more seeds.
  (*a*) Seeds, two or more, and in distinct cells (Apple, Shadbush). A pome. Go to 1.
  (*a*) Seed, one to many, not in distinct cells (Huckleberry). A berry. Go to 2.

B. Fleshy (or sometimes nearly dry), with one or more "stones." A drupe or an etærio.
  (*a*) Solitary, with one or in Papaw with several large stones (Cherry, Papaw). Go to 3.
  (*a*) Solitary, with one to several small stones (Sumach). Go to 4.
  (*a*) Clustered on one receptacle, each drupelet with one small stone (Raspberry). Go to 5.

C. Not fleshy, with one or in the "samara" sometimes two ripened seeds
  (*a*) The coat dry, tipped with the remains of the style, and free from but enclosing its one small seed (Groundsel Tree). An achenium. Go to 6.
  (*a*) The coat, a thin membrane forming a "wing" around or at the sides of the fruit (Trefoil Maple). A samara. Go to 7.
  (*a*) The coat a cup, a wrap, or a scale (Acorn, Hazel-nut, Alder). A glans, a nut, or a nutlet. Go to 8.

CLASS II.—Fruit releasing the ripened seeds by splitting:

 (*a*) Splitting on one side, one-celled (Spiræa, Shrub Yellow-Root). A follicle. Go to 9.
 (*a*) Splitting on two sides, one-celled, with seeds in one row (False Indigo). A legume. Go to 10.
 (*a*) Any form of dry fruit that splits up and down, and is not otherwise named. A capsule. Go to 11.
 (*a*) A cone-shaped aggregation of capsules (Sweet-Bay). A cone of capsules. Go to 12.

NOTE.—Names in *italics* are repetitions made because of real or apparent resemblance to the class with which they are placed.

1

Roses (apparently pomes, really acheniums), page 80.
Chokeberry, page 100.
Dogberry, page 102.
Thorns (Cratægus), page 104.
Shad-Bush, page 108.
Sweet-scented Shrub, page 110.

2

Barberry (oblong, red, one to few-seeded), page 38.
Gooseberries, page 114.
Currants, page 118.
Elders (three-seeded), page 130.
Snowberries (snow-white, two-seeded), page 144.
Wolfberry (white, two-seeded, page 144.
Indian Currant (dark-red, two-seeded), page 146.
Fly Honeysuckles (several seeded), page 146.
Huckleberries (ten-seeded), page 156.
Blueberries (many-seeded), page 162.

Deerberry (many-seeded), page 160.
Bilberries (many-seeded) page 164.
Privet (two to four-seeded) page 190.
Shepherdia (one seed), page 198.
Mistletoe (one seed), page 199.
Yew (red, one seed), page 232.
Juniper (one to three seeds) page 230.

3

Papaw, page 38.
Plums, page 81.
Choke-Cherry, page 84.
Viburnums, page 136.
Fringe-Tree, page 190.
Spice-Bush, page 194.
Leatherwood, page 196.
Daphne, page 198.
Buffalo-Nut, page 200.

4

Ilexes (stones four to eight), page 54.
Mt. Holly (stones four to five), page 56.

Fruit

Buckthorns (stones two to three), page 61.
Sumachs (stone one) page 70.
Ivies (stone one) page 76.
Thorns (Cratægus, stones one to five), page 104.
Angelica Tree (stones five), page 122.
Dogwoods (Cornels, stones two), page 126.
Viburnums (stone one), page 134.
Fringe-Tree (stone one), page 190.
Mistletoe (stone one), page 199.
Sweet-Gale (stone one), page 204.
Bayberry (stone one), page 202.
Sweet-Fern (stone one), page 205.
Broom Crow-Berry (minute stones three to four), page 226.
Black Crow-Berry (stones six to nine), page, 228.
American Yew (red, stone one), page 232.

5

Raspberries, page 90.
Thimbleberry, page 92.
Blackberries, page 94.

6

Roses (apparently a pome), page 80.
Sweet-scented Shrub (apparently a pome), page 110.
Marsh Elder, page 154.
Groundsel Tree, page 154.
Shepherdia (apparently a berry), page 198.

7

Shrubby Trefoil, page 50.
Mountain Maple, page 60.

8

Birches (scale-like nutlets), page 206.
Alders (scale-like nutlets), page 209.
Hazel-nuts, page 212.
Hornbeam, page 214.
Oak, page 206.
Dwarf Chestnut, page 218.

9

Shrub, Yellow-Root, page 34.
Spiræas, page 86.
Nine-Bark, page 88.

10

Hudsonias (two to six-seeded), page 42.
Prickly Ash (one to two-seeded), page 47.
False Indigo (two-seeded), page 78.
Lead-Plant (one-seeded), page 78.

11

St.-John's-worts (one to five-celled, many-seeded), page 44.
Prickly Ash, (one-celled, one to two-seeded), page 47.
Burning-Bush (three to five-celled, few-seeded), page 58.
Strawberry-Bush (three to five-celled, few-seeded), page 60.
Bladder-Nut (three-celled, three to twelve-seeded), page 68.
New Jersey Tea (three-celled, three-seeded), page 64.
Narrow-leaved Ceanothus (three-celled, three-seeded), page 64.

- Wild Hydrangea (two-beaked, two-celled in lower part, many-seeded), page 111.
- Itea (two-celled, eight to twelve-seeded), page 112.
- Witch-hazel (two-celled, two-seeded), page 118.
- Bush Honeysuckle (two, apparently four-celled, many-seeded), page 150.
- Button-Bush (two- to four-celled, two- to four-seeded), page 152.
- Andromedas (five-celled, many-seeded), page 166.
- Leucòthoë (five-celled, many-seeded), page 169.
- Leather-Leaf, five-celled, many-seeded) page 171.
- Laurels (Kálmia, five-celled, many-seeded), page 174.
- Rhododendrons (five-celled, many-seeded), page 182.
- Labrador Tea (five-celled, many-seeded), page 186.
- Sweet Pepper-Bush (three-celled, many-seeded), page 188.
- Willows (one-celled, many-seeded), page 220.

12

Sweet-Bay, page 36.

DESCRIPTION OF SHRUBS
(With Illustrations)

CLASS FIRST
(Angiospermæ)

Division I
PETALS MOSTLY NOT UNITED
(Polypetalous)

1. Family RANUNCULACEÆ. (Crowfoot Fam.)

Genus XANTHORHIZA. (Marshall.)

From two Greek words meaning "yellow" and "root."

Fig. 1.—Shrub Yellow-Root. *X. apiifòlia, L'Her.*

Flowers, small, dark purple, in slender drooping clusters, appearing with the leaves. *Petals*, five, not united, much smaller than the five sepals, slightly two-lobed, raised on a claw. *Stamens*, five to ten. *Seed-cases*, free from the sepals.

Leaves, once or twice compound (odd-feathered). *Leaflets*, three to five, stemless, lobed and toothed, and two to three inches in length.

Bark and Roots, bitter, deep yellow.

Fruit, in clusters, oblong, one-celled, one-seeded; splitting once lengthwise; about one eighth of an inch long; a follicle.

Found, along shady banks of streams in Pennsylvania Southwestern New York, and Kentucky, and southward among the mountains.

A bushy plant, two to three feet high. A yellow dye is made from its roots.

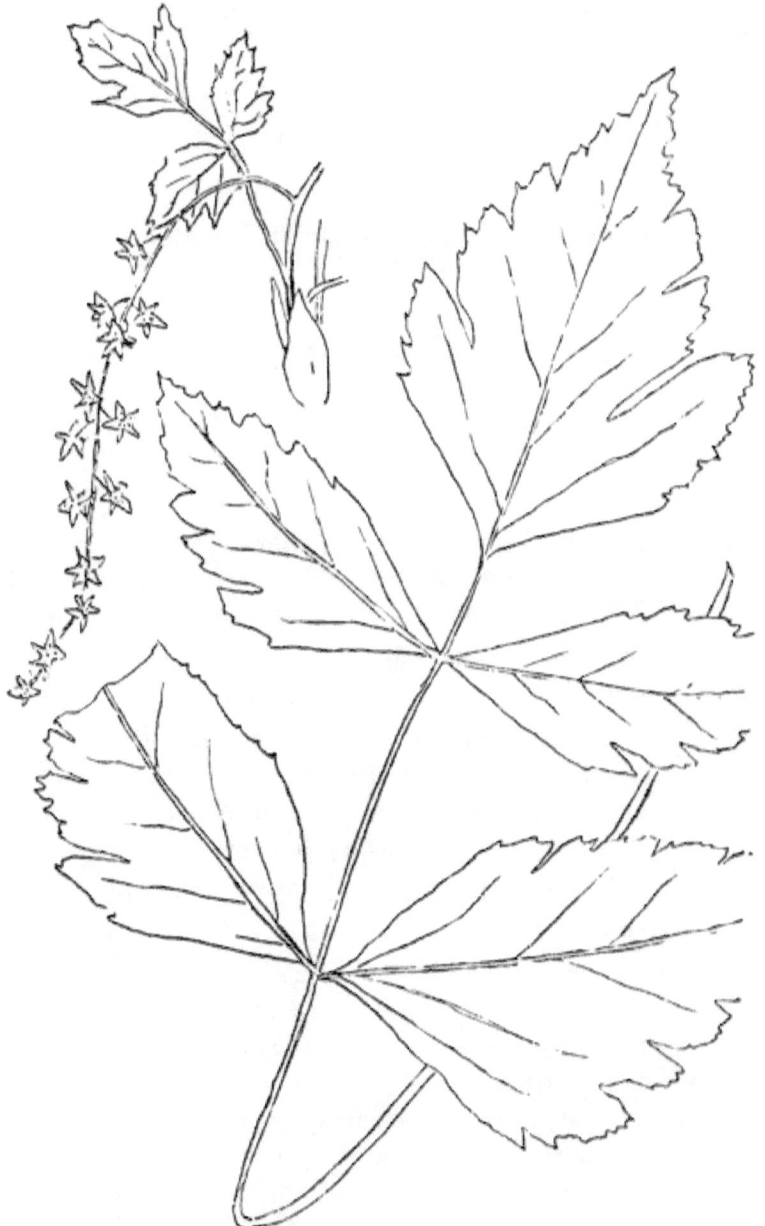

Fig. 1.—Shrub Yellow-Root. (**Xanthorhiza apiifòlia**, L'Her.) Leaf, and spray of flowers with young leaf.

2. Family MAGNOLIACEÆ. (Magnolia Fam.)

Genus MAGNOLIA, L. (Magnolia.)

From "Magnol," the name of a botanist of the 17th century.

Fig. 2.—Sweet-Bay. Swamp Laurel. Small Magnolia.
M. Virginiana, L. (M. glauca, L.)

Flowers, solitary, at the ends of the branches, two to three inches across, white, very fragrant. *Petals*, six to nine, not united. *Sepals*, three, colored like the petals. *Stamens*, more than ten. *Seed-cases*, many, free from the sepals, mostly clinging together over the lengthened receptacle. June to August.

Leaves, three to six inches long, simple, alternate, edge entire, thick and smooth, dark-green and polished above, white below, the mid-vein green and distinct, the side veins indistinct.

Bark, smoothish, light-gray, aromatic, and bitter.

Fruit, an oblong cone, fleshy or somewhat woody, red. When mature the cells of this "cone" split, and the enclosed bright-red seeds (one or two to each cell) drop out and hang suspended by delicate spiral threads. An aggregation of capsules. September.

Found, in swampy ground, from Massachusetts southward, oftenest near the coast.

A bush, or sometimes a small tree, four to twenty-five feet high. Southward it is often still higher, and its leaves are evergreen. All parts of the bush, as in the other magnolias, have an intensely bitter aromatic juice. "The fresh bark has long been considered as a bitter, aromatic tonic and gentle laxative." "The bark, cones, and seeds have been used medicinally from the time of the aborigines, especially against rheumatism and as an antiperiodic." In wet ground it can be successfully cultivated.

Fig. 2.—Sweet-Bay. (M. Virginiàna, L.) (a) Flower. (b) Fruit.

3. Family ANONACEÆ. (Papaw Fam.)

Genus ASIMINA, ADAMS. (Papaw.)

Fig. 3.—**Papaw Custard-Apple.** *A. triloba (L.), Dunal.*

Flowers, one and a half inches across; dull purple, in drooping clusters, appearing with the leaves. *Petals*, six, thick, in two rows, not united. *Sepals*, three. *Stamens*, numerous in a rounded mass. *Seed-cases*, few, free from the sepals. March, April.

Leaves, simple, alternate, edge entire, five to ten inches long, reverse egg-shape. *Apex*, pointed or sometimes rounded. *Base*, taper-pointed, or slightly rounded; thin, rusty-downy when young, soon becoming smooth and polished.

Bark, silvery-gray, smooth and polished; young shoots downy.

Fruit, about three inches long by one and one half inches thick, egg-shape, yellow, pulpy, about ten-seeded; of disagreeable odor when green; sweet and edible after frost, when it turns black without and within, and becomes in color and consistency almost custard-like. October.

Found, from western New York to Southern Iowa, and southward.

A bush or small tree of unpleasant odor when bruised; densely clothed with long leaves.

4. Family BERBERIDÀCEÆ. (Barberry Fam.)

Genus BÉRBERIS, L. (Barberry.)

From the Arabic name of the fruit.

Fig. 4.—**Barberry.** *B. vulgàris, L.*

Flowers, yellow, drooping, in many-blossomed clusters. *Petals*, six, not united, reverse egg-shape, concave,

Fig. 3.—Papaw. A. triloba (L.), Dunal.

(a) Flower. (b) Fruit, two-thirds natural size.

Barberry (Berberidaceæ)

with two glandular spots on the inside of each near the base. *Sepals*, six (with two to six small bracts beneath), rounded, attached beneath the seed-case. *Stamens*, six, irritable, opposite the petals. *Seed-case*, one, free. May, June.

Leaves, simple, alternate or often clustered in rosettes; edge finely toothed, each tooth tipped with a delicate bristle; sour. On the new shoots the leaves often take the form of branching spines.

Wood and inner bark yellow.

Fruit, in drooping clusters, scarlet, oblong, with one to few seeds; edible, but too acid to be agreeable excepting in "preserve"; a berry. September.

Found in thickets in fields and along roadsides; abundantly in New England, where it has become thoroughly naturalized since its introduction from Europe, less commonly elsewhere.

A curious thorny bush, three to eight feet high, with bluish-green foliage, attractive in flower and more attractive in fruit. The bark and roots, used with alum, yield a yellow dye.

In some regions, an old opinion is said still to linger, — that the presence of the barberry causes blight in the grain field.

There is a curious fact reported concerning the flowers which is suggestive of human nerves. When not "doctored," the least touch upon one of their stamens will cause it to spring like a tiny thread of steel, but treat the bush with laudanum or any opiate and the stamens become limp, or with a poison like arsenic and they become rigid, as wholly irresponsive in either case as would be a human nerve.

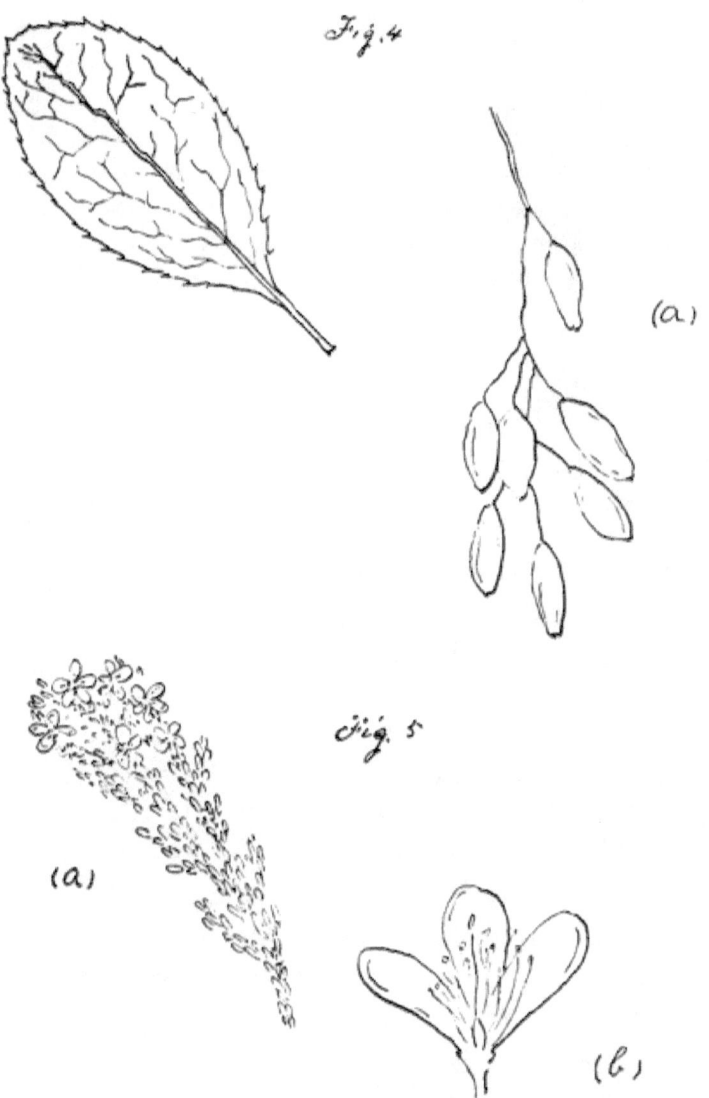

Fig. 4.—Barberry. (B. vulgàris, L.) (a) Fruit.

Fig. 5.—Hudsònia. (H. tomentòsa, Nutt.) (a) Flowering branch. (b) Section of flower, enlarged.

The peculiar spring arrangement of the stamens helps to secure the desirable cross-fertilization of the flower. The honey being between the base of the stamens and the seed-case, when an insect in searching for the sweets touches a stamen he "springs" it. Thereupon he receives a smart rap and a dusting from the pollen-covered anther, and so is frightened away to other flowers.

5. Family CISTACEÆ.   (Rock-rose Fam.)

Genus HUDSÒNIA, L.   (Hudsonia.)

From the name of an early English botanist.

Fig. 5.—**Hudsònia**.   *H. tomentòsa, Nutt.*

Flowers, bright-yellow, small, with stalks sometimes present and short, but usually wanting, crowded along the upper parts of the branches. *Petals*, five, not united, lasting only for a day. *Sepals*, five, two of them minute, and all of them much smaller than the petals. *Stamens*, nine to thirty. *Style*, long and slender. *Seed-case*, one, free, with one cell and two to six seeds. May to June.

Leaves, scale-like, about one twelfth of an inch long, closely pressed to the branches and covering them, downy and whitish.

Fruit, oblong, one-celled, two- to six-seeded, enclosed in the calyx. A pod.

Found, on sandy shores from Maine to Maryland and along the great lakes westward to Minnesota.

A very bushy heath-like little shrub, usually less than one foot high, and oftenest found growing in thick, matted patches.

Fig. 6.—St.-Peter's-wort. (A. stans, Michx.)
Fig. 7.—Shrubby St.-John's-wort, L. (Hypericum prolificum, L.)

St.-John's-wort (*Hypericàceæ*)

Hudsònia. *H. ericòides, L.*

This species differs from the preceding chiefly in these items:

Flowers, on smooth slender stalks.

Leaves, greenish, one sixth to one third of an inch long, and spreading from the branch.

Found, along the coast from Maine to Virginia.

6. Family HYPERICACEÆ. (St.-John's-wort Fam.)

Flowers, yellow. *Petals,* four or five, not united. *Sepals,* four or five. *Stamens,* many. *Seed-case,* one, free, one- to five-celled; many-seeded.

Leaves, simple, opposite, entire, dotted when held to the light or under the lens. *Stipules,* none.

Fruit, dry, one- to five-celled, splitting lengthwise, a many-seeded capsule.

A Guide to the Genera.

Petals, four; Sepals four, in very unequal pairs. (1) Áscyrum (St. Peter's-wort.)
"   five;   "   five, alike   (2) Hypéricum (St. John's-wort.)

(1) Genus ÁSCYRUM, L. (St. Peter's-wort.)

From two Greek terms meaning "without" and "roughness."

Fig. 6.—St.-Peter's-wort. *A. stans, Michx.*

Flowers, usually three together, showy, at the ends of the branches. *Petals,* reverse egg-shape; the two larger sepals round, about one half inch across; the smaller ones lance-shaped. *Styles,* three or four. *Seed-case,* with one cell. June to August:

Leaves, ten twelfths to one and one fourth inches long, one third as wide, stemless, rather thick, oval or oblong, somewhat clasping around the branch.

St.-John's-wort (Hypericaceæ)

Branches, two-edged, erect.

Fruit, splitting into two to four pieces.

Found, in pine barrens from Long Island to Pennsylvania and southward.

A small, stout shrub, with stem erect and straight, one to two feet high, and branching above.

Saint Andrew's Cross. *A. Crux-Andreæ, L.*

Flowers, one to three in a leafy cluster at the ends of the branches. *Petals*, oblong. Outer *sepals*, oval and twice as long as the flower-stem, the inner ones minute. *Styles*, two. *Seed-case*, with one cell.

Leaves, one half to one inch long, stemless, thin, narrowly reverse egg-shape, narrowed to the base. Branches two-edged toward their ends, drooping.

Fruit, splitting into two to four pieces.

Found, in Nantucket, and from the pine barrens of New Jersey westward and southward.

A drooping shrub, one to two feet high, with many branches.

(2) Genus HYPÉRICUM, Tourn. (St.-John's-wort.)

In the old mythology the St.-John's-wort was dedicated to Baldur, the Sun God, on account of its golden flowers. When the old religion gave way to Christianity, Baldur's Day became St.-John's-day, and Baldur's flower St. John's flower.

The genus was once in high repute for its supposed ability to guard against evil spirits, and for other magical powers. On this account the various species were often planted around dwellings. In Scotland the plant is said still to be carried as a charm; and in France and Germany, on the day of the nativity of St. John the Baptist, the peasantry trim their homes with it in honor of the saint, and to gain his favor.

> "I must gather the mystic St.-John's-wort to-night,
> The wonderful herb whose leaf will decide
> If the coming year shall make me a bride."
> *Translated from the German.*

> "Trefoil, Vervain, *John's-wort*, Dill,
> Hinder witches of their will."

Fig. 7.—Shrubby St.-John's-wort. *H. prolificum, L.*

Flowers, orange-yellow, three quarters of an inch across, crowded in simple or compound leafy clusters. *Stamens,* very numerous. *Seed-case,* three-celled. *Styles,* three more or less united. July, August.

Leaves, one to two and one half inches long, narrow; edge often wavy; apex usually obtuse; base narrowed.

Branchlets, two-edged.

Fruit, one third to one half inch long.

Found, from New Jersey to Michigan and southward.

A very ornamental little shrub, usually two to four feet in height, but variable in size.

Hypéricum densiflòrum. *Pursh.*

This species differs from the preceding chiefly in these items:

Flowers, one half to two thirds of an inch in diameter, in crowded compound clusters.

Leaves, about one inch in length.

Fruit, one third to one quarter inch in length.

Found, from the pine barrens of New Jersey to Kentucky and Arkansas, and southward.

Kalm's St.-John's-wort. *H. Kalmianum, L.*

Flowers, one inch across, three to seven in a close cluster.

Styles, five. *Seed-case*, five-celled.

Leaves, one to two inches long, crowded and narrow.

Branches, somewhat four-sided, with two of the edges slightly winged.

Fruit, egg-shape.

Found, on wet rocks at Niagara Falls, and among the northern lakes.

7. Family RUTACEÆ. (Rue Fam.)

Flowers, small, greenish-white, in clusters; sometimes taking the staminate and the pistillate forms on different shrubs. *Petals*, three to five, not united. *Sepals*, three to five, or wanting. *Stamens*, in the staminate flowers, as many as the petals and alternate with them; in the pistillate flowers, either imperfect or wanting. *Seed-cases*, one to five, free from the calyx.

Leaves, compound, alternate, dotted when held to the light; edge of leaflets entire or nearly so. *Stipules*, none.

Bark, pungent or bitter.

Fruit, one- to two-seeded, one-celled, splitting into two pieces, thick and fleshy, a fleshy pod; or two-celled, two-seeded, thin, and winged all around; a samara.

GUIDE TO THE GENERA.

Stems prickly; Seed-cases three to five, separate.　(1) Xanthoxylum (Prickly Ash).
Stems not prickly; Seed-case, one with two cells.　(2) Ptelea (Shrubby Trefoil).

(1) Genus XANTHOXYLUM, L. (Prickly Ash.)

From two Greek words meaning "yellow" and "wood."

Fig. 8. Northern Prickly Ash.   Toothache Tree.
X. Americanum, Mill.

Flowers, in small, dense clusters at the sides of the branches, appearing before the leaves, and sometimes taking the pistillate form on one tree, and the staminate on another. *Petals*, four to five. *Sepals*, four to five, or obsolete. *Seed-cases*, three to five, separate, but with their slender styles more or less united. April, May.

Leaves, alternate. *Leaflets*, in two to four pairs, with an odd one at the end; edges entire or nearly so; surface smooth above (or when young, downy), downy beneath.

Branches, and often the leaf-stalks armed with short, stout, brown prickles.

Fruit, thick and fleshy, one-celled, splitting lengthwise into two parts; one- to two-seeded. *Seeds*, black, smooth, and shining.

Found, in rocky woods, and along river banks; often forming thickets; common, especially northward.

A shrub four to twelve feet high, or in cultivation sometimes twenty feet high. All its parts are bitter and aromatic. The leaves furnish a home remedy for rheumatism, toothache, etc. When crushed they yield a strong lemon odor, due to an oil contained in the transparent dots. The bush serves well for hedges.

It is said that the Indians use the prickly ash as a medicine under the name of Hantola; that they chew the bark for aching teeth; make decoctions, mostly of the roots, for rheumatism and colic; and, mixed with bear's grease, use it for poultices.

In typhoid cases the tincture of the berry is considered very helpful. "In typhus fever, typhus pneumonia, and typhoid conditions generally, I am compelled to say that I consider the tincture of prickly-ash berries superior to any other kind of medicine."—DR. KING as quoted by Millspaugh.

Rue (Rutaceæ)

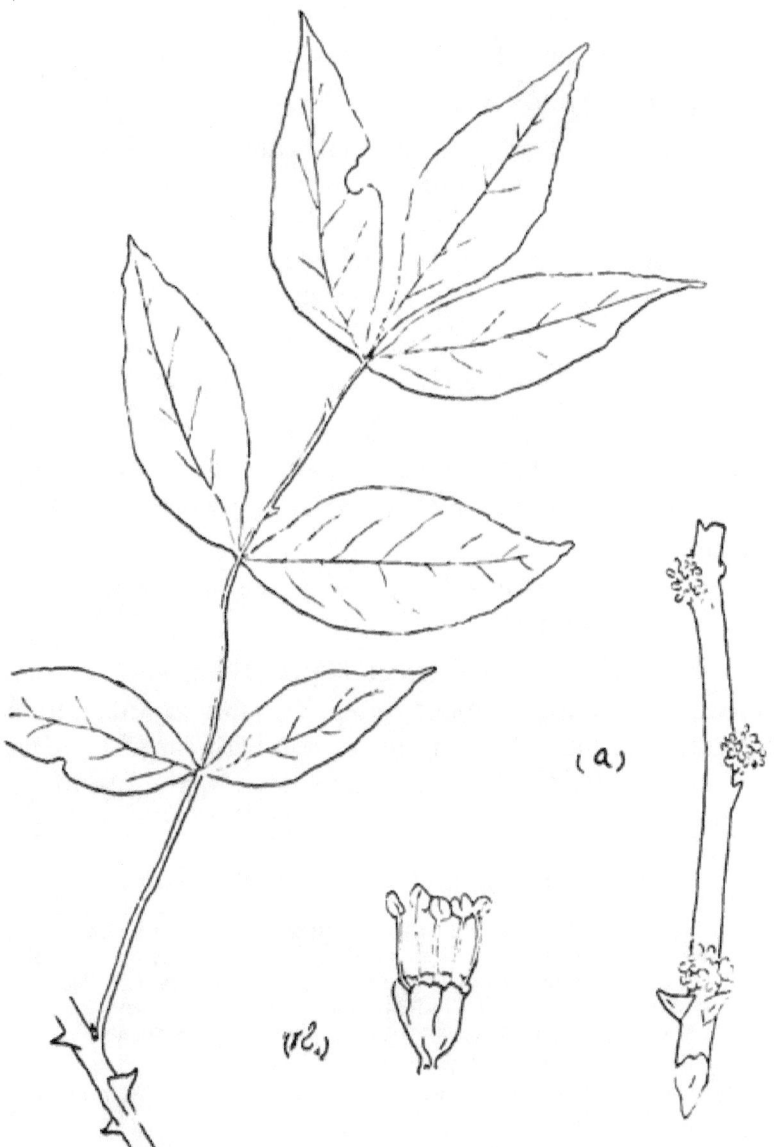

Fig. 8.—Prickly Ash. (X. Americànum, Mill.)
(*a*) Flowering twig. (*b*) Staminate flower, enlarged.

(2) Genus PTELEA, L.   (Shrubby Trefoil.)

From the Greek name of the elm, given because of the similarity of the fruits.

Fig. 9.—Shrubby Trefoil.   Hop Tree.   *P. trifoliáta, L.*

Flowers, of marked odor, in small compound clusters at the ends of the young branches. Staminate, pistillate, and perfect flowers sometimes form on the same bush.   *Petals*, sepals, and stamens three to five.   *Seed-case*, two-celled.   *Style*, short.   June.

Leaves, of three leaflets, two to four inches long, with edges entire or nearly so, and downy when young.

Fruit, "orbicular," two-celled, two-seeded, with the edge broadly winged throughout; nearly one inch across; intensely bitter, and used as a substitute for hops; a samara.

Found, in rocky places from Long Island to Minnesota, and southward.

A shrub six to eight feet high, well fitted for ornament, being neat in appearance, not liable to attack from insects, and hung late in the season with large bunches of hop-like fruit.   Its leaves and flowers are late in unfolding.

8. Family ILICÍNEÆ.   (Holly Fam.)

Flowers, in staminate and pistillate forms, white or greenish, small, along the sides of the branches (axillary.) *Petals*, four to eight, separate, or slightly united at the base. *Calyx*, minute. *Stamens*, as many as the petals, and alternate with them. *Seed-case*, free from the calyx, four- to eight-celled, four- to eight-seeded.

Leaves, simple, alternate, edge-toothed or entire.

Fruit, berry-like drupes about the size of peas, with four to eight stones.

GUIDE TO THE GENERA.

Petals oval or reverse egg-shape ; Leaves toothed.   (1) Ìlex (Holly, etc.).
Petals narrow and pointed ; Leaves entire (or sometimes slightly toothed).   (2) Nemopánthes (Mt. Holly).

Fig. 9.—Hop Tree. (P. trifoliàta, L.)
(a) Fruit. (b) Staminate flower, enlarged.

Holly (Ilicineæ)

(1) Genus Ìlex, L. (Holly, etc.)

Fig. 10.—Ìlex montàna, T. and G. *I. monticola, G.*

Flowers, with their parts in fours or fives (or rarely in sixes). *Sepals*, delicately fringed with fine hairs. Staminate flowers usually in clusters; pistillate usually solitary, with very short stems.

Leaves, three to five inches long, egg-shape or long oval, sharply toothed, mostly smooth. *Apex* and base, pointed.

Fruit, the size of a pea; fleshy, red or purple. *Nutlets*, four to six, each finely lined along the back; a drupe.

Found, in damp woods in the Catskill and Tahonic Mountains, and in Cattaraugus County, N. Y., through Pennsylvania as far east as Northampton County, and southward along the Alleghanies.

A shrub sometimes taking the size and shape of a small tree.

Soft Ilex. *I. mollis, Gray.*

This species quite closely resembles the preceding, except in these items:

Flowers, the staminate clusters with very many blossoms.

Leaves, soft, downy beneath.

Found, in Burgoons Gap, Alleghanies of Pennsylvania, and along the mountains in the Southern States.

Fig. 11.—**Winterberry. Black Alder.** *I. verticillàta (L.), Gray.*

Flowers, the staminate in stemless clusters, with the parts in fours, fives, or sixes; the pistillate, solitary or clustered, with the parts in sixes (or rarely in fives, sevens, or eights). *Flower-stems*, all very short. July.

Holly (Ilicineæ)

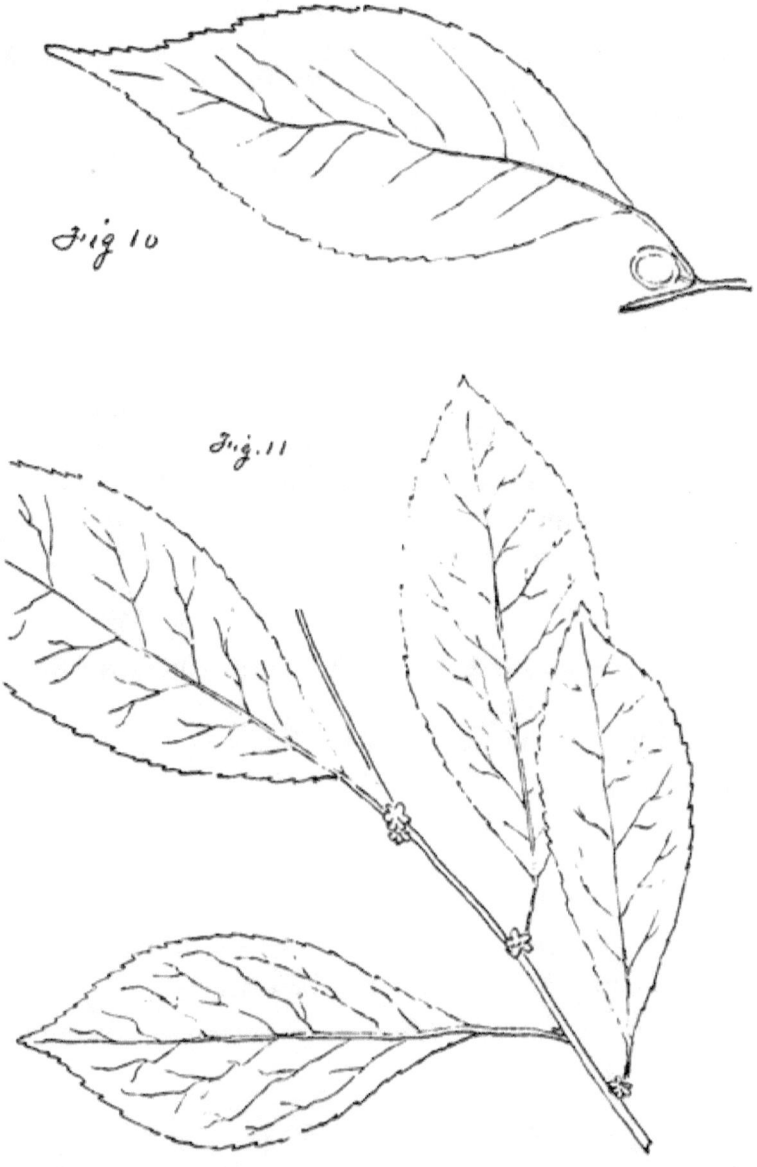

Fig. 10.—Ilex. (I. montàna, G. and T.)
Fig. 11.—Winterberry. I. verticillàta (L.), G.

Holly (Ilicineæ)

Leaves, variable, reverse egg-shape to oval and wedge-shape, downy beneath, especially along the vines, strongly net-veined. *Apex* and base pointed. *Leaf-stems*, short.

Fruit, about the size of a small pea, fleshy, bright red. *Nutlets*, six to eight, smooth, moon-shape, often continuing in place long after the leaves have fallen; a drupe. September, October.

Found, in moist woods or swamps; common.

A shrub, usually about eight feet high; very noticeable among the autumn trees and bushes because of its show of fiery-red berries. Its bark is tonic, astringent, and antiseptic, and is often used with the effect of Peruvian bark in intermittent fevers. "It is probably as well known to domestic practice as any indigenous shrub."

Smooth Winterberry. *I. lævigàta (Pursh.)*, Gray.

This species differs from the last chiefly in these items:

Flowers, the staminate forms on stems nearly one inch long. June.

Leaves, shining above, smooth beneath, and only minutely downy on the veins. *Leaf-stems*, one half to five sixths of an inch long.

Fruit, larger than the last (about one third inch in diameter) and ripening earlier. September.

Found, in wet ground from the mountains of Virginia northward.

Fig. 12.—Inkberry. *I. glàbra (L.)*, Gray.

Flowers, small and white, with the parts mostly in sixes; the staminate blossoms in a three- to six-flowered

Holly (Ilicineæ)

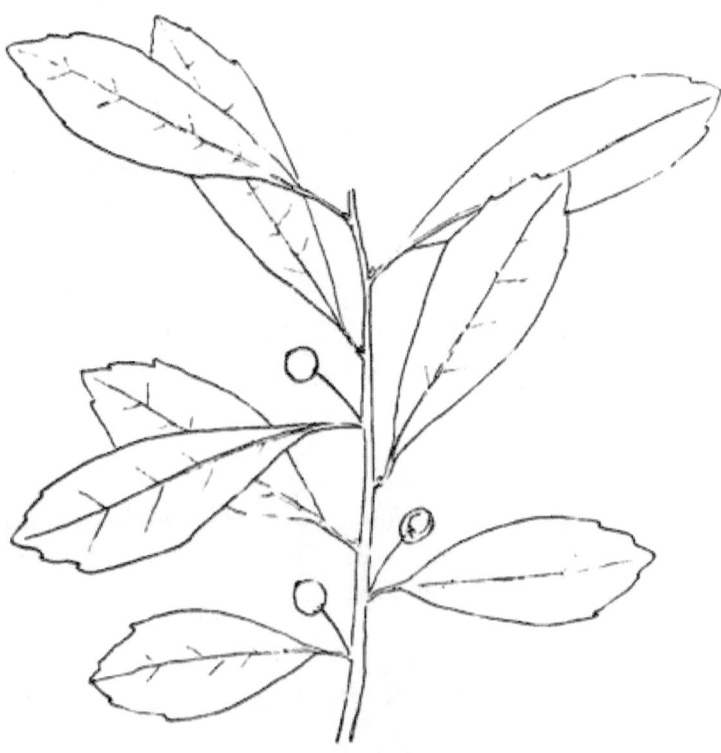

Fig. 12.—Inkberry. I. glàbra (L.), G.

cluster, the fertile ones usually solitary. *Flower-stem*, about one half inch long, slender, and minutely hairy. June.

Leaves, one to one and three quarter inches long, thick, dark, and very shiny above, both surfaces smooth, veins beneath scarcely perceptible; wedge-shape or oblong, notched toward the apex, with a few (usually five) remote teeth.

Fruit, the size of a small pea in the axils of the leaves, round, black, shining, often remaining through the winter; not edible. *Stones*, four to six, smooth; a berry-like drupe.

Found, in sandy and low ground from Cape Ann, Massachusetts, southward near the coast.

A pretty evergreen shrub two to four feet high, well worthy of cultivation because of its neat shape and shining evergreen leaves.

It is considered of value medicinally (in fevers), but its chief use is for decoration. Quantities of it are sent from the southern counties of New Jersey to the New York florists, who easily keep it in good condition for several months.

(2) Genus NEMOPÁNTHES, Raf.

Probably from the Greek words meaning "thread," "foot," and "flower," in reference to the thread-like stalk of the blossom.

Fig. 13.—Mountain Holly. *N. mucronàta (L.), Trelease. N. fasciculàris, Raf.*

Flowers, usually solitary, small, greenish-white, on long, slender stems. *Petals*, four or five, narrow, pointed, as long as the stamens, separate. *Sepals*, in the staminate flowers in the form of minute teeth; in the

Holly (Ilicineæ)

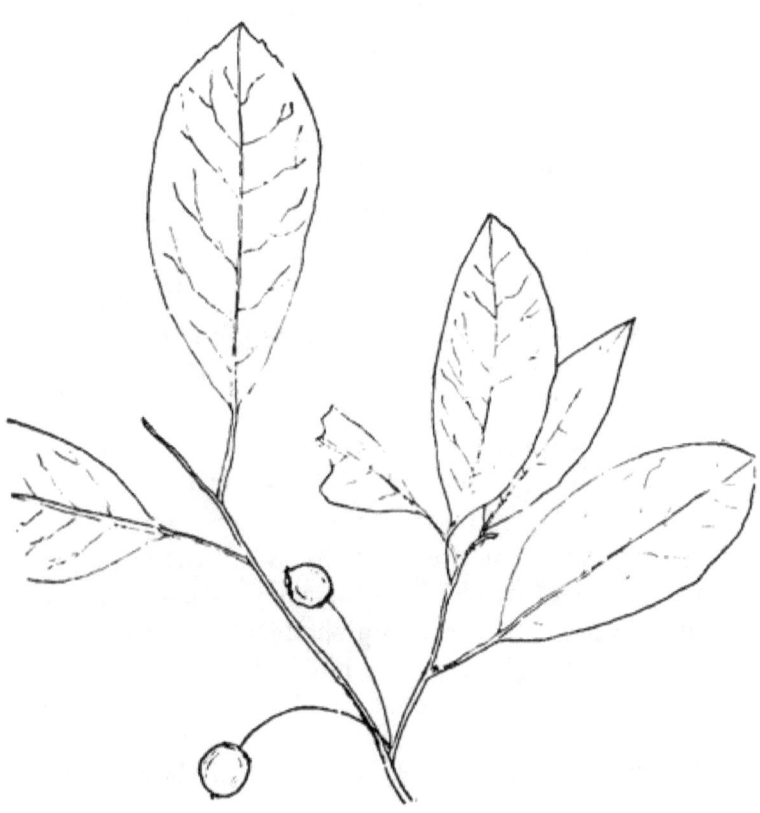

Fig. 13.—Mountain Holly. N. mucronàta (L.) Trelease.

pistillate only rudimentary. *Stamens*, four or five, with slender filaments. *Seed-case*, hemispherical. May, June.

Leaves, one to two inches long, egg-shape to reverse egg-shape, edge entire, or sometimes slightly toothed; smooth. *Leaf-stem*, slender.

Fruit, the size of a pea, red, nearly round, on slender stems. *Nutlets*, four or five, somewhat angular; a berry-like drupe. August.

Found, in damp ground from the mountains of Virginia northward.

A much-branched shrub four to eight feet high, with smooth ash-gray bark; the young shoots purple or olive, with round gray dots.

I found the pretty bush first on an open, rocky point in Lake Placid, among the Adirondacks. It was set thick with bright red berries, and its whole aspect, owing to the toughening of the wind and sun, was tangled and "chunky." Afterward I found it where it had been more delicately reared, in the damp shade of the neighboring woods, with straighter and slimmer branches, and paler foliage.

9. Family CELASTRACEÆ. (Staff-Tree Fam.)

Genus EUÓNYMUS, Tourn. (Burning-Bush, etc.)

From two Greek words meaning "good" and "name."

Fig. 14.—Burning-Bush. Waahoo. Spindle-Tree.
E. atropurpureus, Jacq.

Flowers, dark purple, small, regular in loose clusters of three to six blossoms, at the sides of the branches; the parts of the flower commonly in fours. *Stamens*,

Staff-Tree (Celastràceæ)

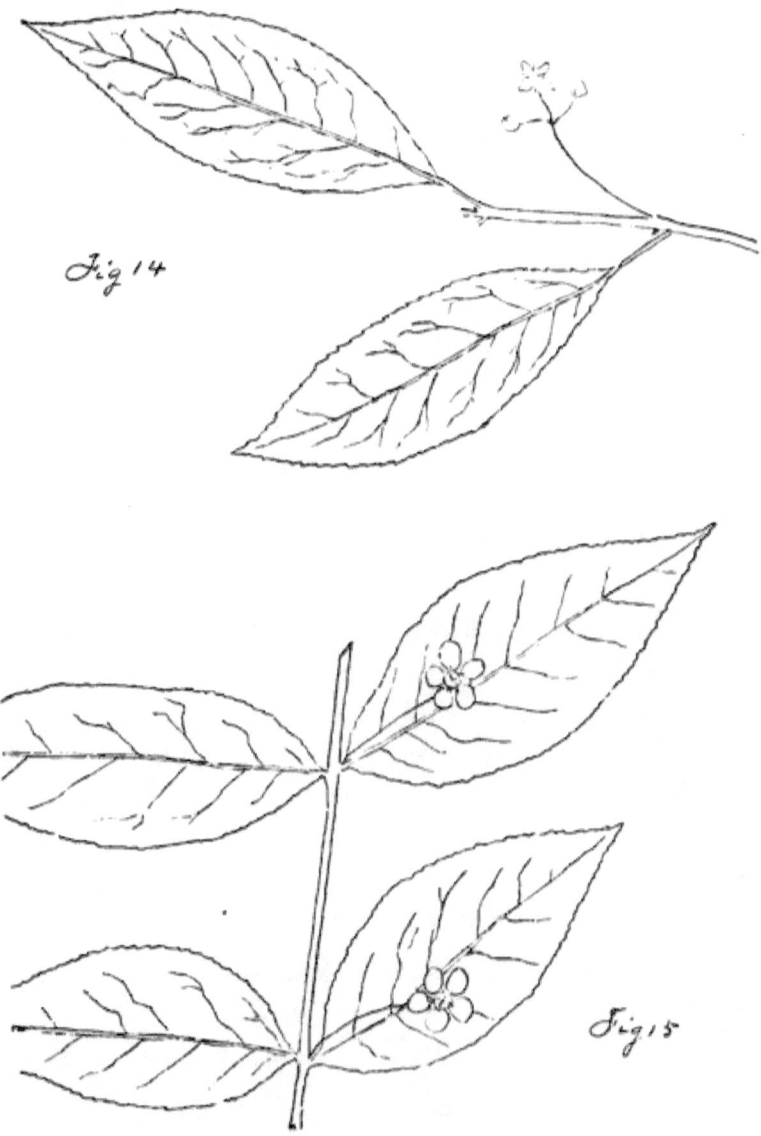

Fig. 14.—Burning-Bush. (E. atropurpùreus, Jacq.)
Fig. 15. Strawberry-Bush. (E. Americànus, L.)

Staff-Tree (Celastràceæ)

very short, alternating with the petals, and inserted on a disk which occupies the lower part of the calyx, and is stretched over the seed-case, partly adhering to it. *Seed-case*, free from the calyx, two to five-celled, with one to four seeds in each cell. *Style*, short or none. *Stem*, of the flower-clusters, slender, one to two and one half inches long. June

Leaves, two to five inches long, simple, opposite, toothed, variable in shape, oval and oblong to reverse egg-shape. *Leaf-stem*, one half to one inch long. *Branchlets*, four-sided.

Fruit, very showy, smooth, deeply lobed; when ripe splitting up and down into three to five valves, and so showing the bright red covers of the seeds within. *Cells*, three to five. *Seeds*, few (one to four in each cell), elliptical; a capsule.

Found, in shady woods widely distributed, and in cultivation.

A smooth-barked shrub, six to seventeen feet high, often cultivated, and very attractive in autumn with its abundant drooping clusters of "burning" berries. A medicine of some repute has been prepared from it called "Waahoo."

Fig. 15.—Strawberry-Bush. *E. Americànus, L.*

This species differs from the last chiefly in the following items:

Flowers, greenish, or greenish-purple, and mostly in fives.

Leaves, one to two inches long, nearly stemless.

Fruit, rough, warty, and depressed. *Seeds*, smaller and egg-shape or oval.

Found, in damp and shady places from New York to Illinois, and southward.

An upright or sometimes straggling shrub, two to five feet high.

10. Family RHAMNACEÆ. (Buckthorn Fam.)

Flowers, greenish or white, small and regular (sometimes with the petals wanting). *Petals*, when present, four to five, not united. *Sepals*, four to five. *Stamens*, of the same number as the petals, and alternate with them. *Seed-case*, free from the calyx, or sometimes united to it, two- to five-celled. *Seeds*, one in each cell. Stamens and petals inserted along the edge of a fleshy disk, which lines the tube of the calyx, and in Ceanothus unites it to the lower part of the seed-case.
Leaves, simple, alternate, fine-toothed.
Fruit, a berry-like drupe or a capsule.

GUIDE TO THE GENERA.

Flowers, greenish; Fruit fleshy and berry-like; a drupe. } (1) Rhamnus (Buckthorns).
Flowers, white; Fruit dry and at length splitting; a capsule. } (2) Ceanothus (New Jersey Tea, etc.).

(1) Genus RHAMNUS, Tourn. (Buckthorns.)

Fig. 16.—Lance-Leaved Buckthorn. *R. lanceolata, Pursh.*

Flowers, yellowish-green, small, at the sides of the branches; found sometimes in two slightly different forms on different bushes, but both forms perfect. *Petals*, four and deeply notched. *Sepals*, four. *Stamens*, four. *Seed-case*, free, two- to four-celled. May.

Leaves, oval and oblong, pointed, or on the flowering shoots sometimes blunted.

Fruit, about the size of a small pea, black and fleshy. *Seeds*, two, deeply grooved; a berry-like drupe.

Found, from Pennsylvania to Illinois and Tennessee, and westward.

A tall, unarmed shrub.

Buckthorn (Rhamnaceæ)

Fig. 17.—Alder-Leaved Buckthorn. *R. alnifolia, L'Her.*

Flowers, greenish, small, in clusters at the sides of the branches; the staminate and the pistillate forms usually found on different bushes. *Petals*, wanting. *Sepals*, five. *Stamens*, five. *Seed-case*, two- to four-celled, free from the calyx. June.

Leaves, one to three inches long, about one half as wide.

Fruit, about as large as a currant, somewhat pear-shape, black and fleshy. *Seeds*, three, deeply grooved along the back; a berry-like drupe.

Found, in rough fields and swamps from Maine to Pennsylvania and Nebraska, and northward; common.

A shrub two to four feet high, without thorns.

Common Buckthorn. [*R. cathártica, L.*]

This species is a native of Europe. It is cultivated widely in the form of thorny hedges, and is occasionally found growing wild in the Eastern States. The leaves are egg-shape; the fruit three- to four-seeded.

As far back as the 13th century it was noticed for its medicinal qualities. During the 16th century all medical writers commented on it. It is now fallen into disuse, its cathartic effect being considered too violent.

Carolina Buckthorn. *R. Caroliniàna, Walt.*

Flowers, greenish, small, perfect; in one form in clusters, in another solitary, with short stem. *Petals*, five. *Sepals*, five. *Seed-case*, free. June.

Leaves, two to five inches long, obscurely toothed, strongly veined.

Fruit, black, fleshy, berry-like. *Seeds*, three, not furrowed; a berry-like drupe.

Buckthorn (Rhamnaceæ)

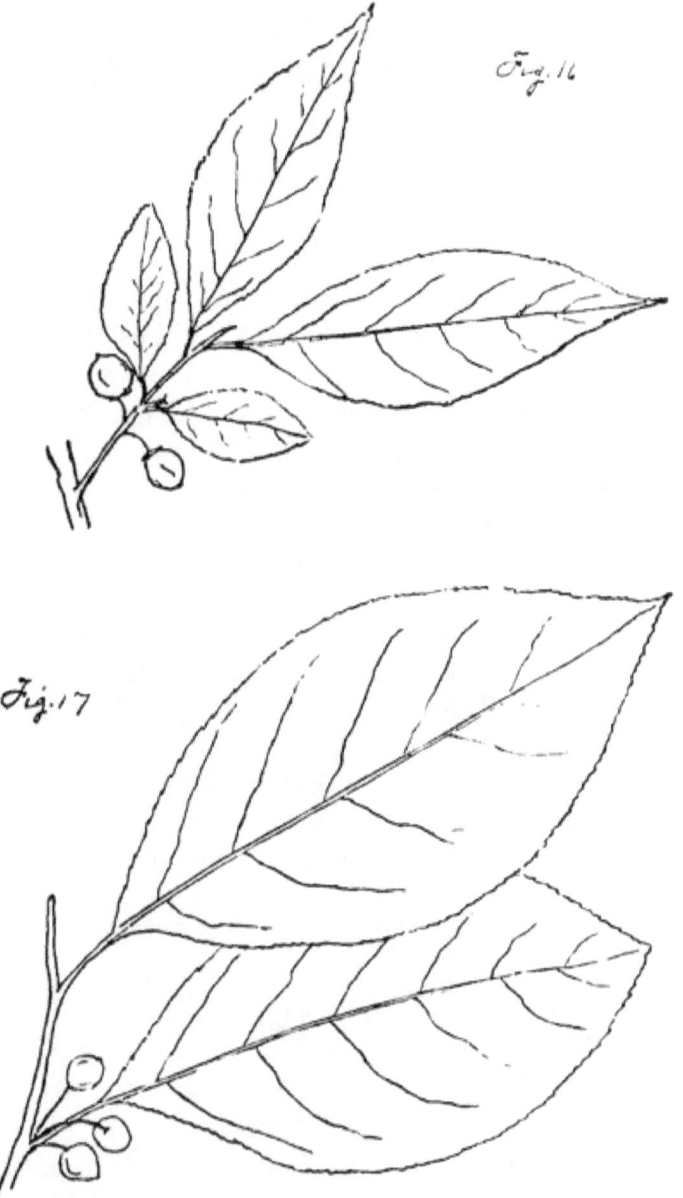

Fig. 16.—Lance-Leaved Buckthorn. (R. lanceolàta, Pursh.)
Fig. 17.—Alder-Leaved Buckthorn. (R. alnifòlia, L'Her.)

Found, in wet places, from New Jersey southward.

A thornless shrub, or sometimes a small tree.

(2) Genus CEANÒTHUS, L.   (New Jersey Tea, etc.)

Fig. 18.—Narrow-Leaved Ceanòthus.   *C. ovàtus, Desf.*

This species differs from the next chiefly in these items:

Flowers, somewhat larger, in nearly hemispherical clusters that are about one and one half inches in diameter. May.

Leaves, narrow oval to narrow egg-shape, usually pointed at both ends, and smooth, or nearly so; the glandular teeth of the edge often black-tipped.

Found, among dry rocks, Western Vermont and Massachusetts, and westward.   It is rare in the East.

Fig. 19.—New Jersey Tea. Red-Root.   *C. Americànus, L.*

Flowers, white, in lengthened clusters at the summit of the flower branches. *Petals*, five, spreading, hooded, attached by slender claws, longer than the calyx. *Calyx*, five-lobed, incurved, the lower part attached with the thick disk to the seed-case, and remaining long after the lobes and the ripened fruit have fallen. Calyx and flower-stem colored like the petals. *Seed-case*, three-celled. July.

Leaves, three quarters to three inches long, egg-shape, dark, dull green; very prominently three-veined from the base, toothed, downy, or often nearly smooth. *Apex*, pointed or obtuse; base often slightly heart-shape.

Fruit, small, dry, three-lobed and three-celled, splitting up and down into three parts. *Seeds*, not furrowed, one in each cell. A capsule.

Fig. 18.—Narrow-Leaved Ceanòthus. (C. ovàtus, Desf.)
(*a*) Flower enlarged.
Fig. 19.—New Jersey Tea. (C. Americànus, L.)
(*b*) Fruit.

Soapberry (Sapindaceæ)

Found, widely distributed in dry woodlands and fields from Canada to Florida.

A shrub one to three feet high, springing from a large dark red root. During the American Revolution and in the Civil War, in some of the Southern States its leaves served for tea. Its root is sometimes used for dyeing.

Common as the shrub is, it was late before I learned to know it; but since that time until now, when it has come to be one of my familiar friends, always the prettiest thing about it has seemed to me to be its quaint and tiny silver-lined cups, emptied of their ripened seeds and shining on their dried stalks among the flowers and leaves of a new year's growth.

It was once widely advertised that the true China tea plant had been discovered in a county of Pennsylvania, and that its identity was certified by an expert from Assam. A company was even formed for its cultivation and sale. The fraud was soon detected; they were using the leaves of the New Jersey tea. An infusion of these leaves tastes like the poorer grades of imported teas, but probably it has none of the tonic effects of real tea.

11. Family SAPINDACEÆ. (Soapberry Fam.)

(1) Genus ACER, Tourn. (Maple.)

Fig. 20.—Mountain Maple. *A. spicàtum, Lam.*

Flowers, greenish, small, regular, crowded in lengthened and upright clusters, which become drooping in fruit; either perfect or in the staminate and pistillate forms on separate plants, appearing after the leaves. *Petals,* narrow, generally five, not united. *Sepals,* of the

Soapberry (Sapindaceæ)

Fig. 20.—Mountain Maple. (A. spicàtum, Lam.)

same number, colored. *Stamens*, six to eight. *Styles*, two, long and slender, and united only below. *Seed-case*, free, two-lobed and two-celled, with two young seeds in each cell (only one ripening). June.

Leaves, simple, opposite, three- (or slightly five-) lobed, the lobes toothed; downy beneath; more or less heart-shaped at base. *Bark*, light gray.

Fruit, in drooping clusters, two-winged, two-seeded; a double samara or "key."

Found, usually in clumps in moist and hilly woods, widely distributed from Maine to Wisconsin, and northward; and southward along the Alleghanies to Virginia and Kentucky.

A shrub six to fifteen feet high, easily distinguished by its bark and leaves from its near relation and frequent neighbor, the Striped Maple (*A. Pennsylvánicum, L.*), which is often of no greater height, though ranked with the trees, and which has a similar liking for damp and hilly woods. The latter has larger and differently shaped leaves (Fig. 74. *Trees of Northeastern America*), and a greenish bark, peculiarly marked lengthwise with stripes.

(2) Genus STAPHYLEA, L. (Bladder-Nut.)

From a Greek word meaning "cluster."

Fig. 21.—American Bladder-Nut. *S. trifolia, L.*

Flowers, white, handsome, in short, drooping clusters at the ends of the branchlets. *Petals*, five, not united. *Stamens*, five, alternating with the petals. *Sepals*, five, whitish. *Styles*, three, lightly united. *Seed-case*, free from the calyx, but with its base slightly sunk in the fleshy receptacle; with three cells, each cell containing several young seeds.

Soapberry (Sapindaceæ)

Fig. 21.—Bladder-Nut. (S. trifòlia, L.)
(*a*) Fruit.

Leaves, compound, opposite; leaflets three to five, toothed, pale beneath, with scattered hairs. *Branches*, greenish-striped.

Fruit, the most remarkable thing about the plant, large, inflated, three-sided, three-parted at the top, three-celled, each cell with one to four smooth, hard seeds, with an odor much like that of a pea-pod. A capsule.

Found, in moist woods and thickets northward from North Carolina and Tennessee.

A handsome shrub, six to ten feet high.

12. Family ANACARDIACEÆ. (Sumach Fam.)

Genus RHUS, L. (Sumachs.)

Possibly from a word meaning "red."

Flowers, greenish, yellowish, or reddish, small, regular, often in the staminate and pistillate forms. *Petals*, five, not united. *Sepals*, five. *Stamens*, five, alternate with the petals. *Styles*, three. *Seed-case*, free, one-celled, with one seed.

Leaves, compound, alternate.

Fruit, nearly round, small, not splitting when ripe, one-seeded. An almost dry drupe.

GUIDE TO THE SPECIES.

(a) Leaflets, more than three.
   (b) Edge of leaflets toothed.
      (c) Leaf stem and branchlets smooth. (1) Smooth Sumach.
      (c) " " " very downy. (2) Stag-Horn Sumach.
   (b) Edge of leaflets entire.
      (c) The common leaf-stem winged between the leaflets. (3) Dwarf Sumach.
      (c) The common leaf-stem not winged. (4) Poison Sumach.
(a) Leaflets, three.
   (b) Edge of leaflets entire, or with a few sharp teeth. (5) Poison Ivy.
   (b) Edge of leaflets with large rounded teeth. (6) Sweet Sumach.

Fig. 22.—(1) **Smooth Sumach.** *R. glabra, L.*

Flowers, small, greenish-red, in dense terminal pyramid-shaped clusters. June, July.

Leaflets, eleven to thirteen, two to three and a half inches long, toothed, pale beneath. *Leaf-stem* and branchlets, smooth.

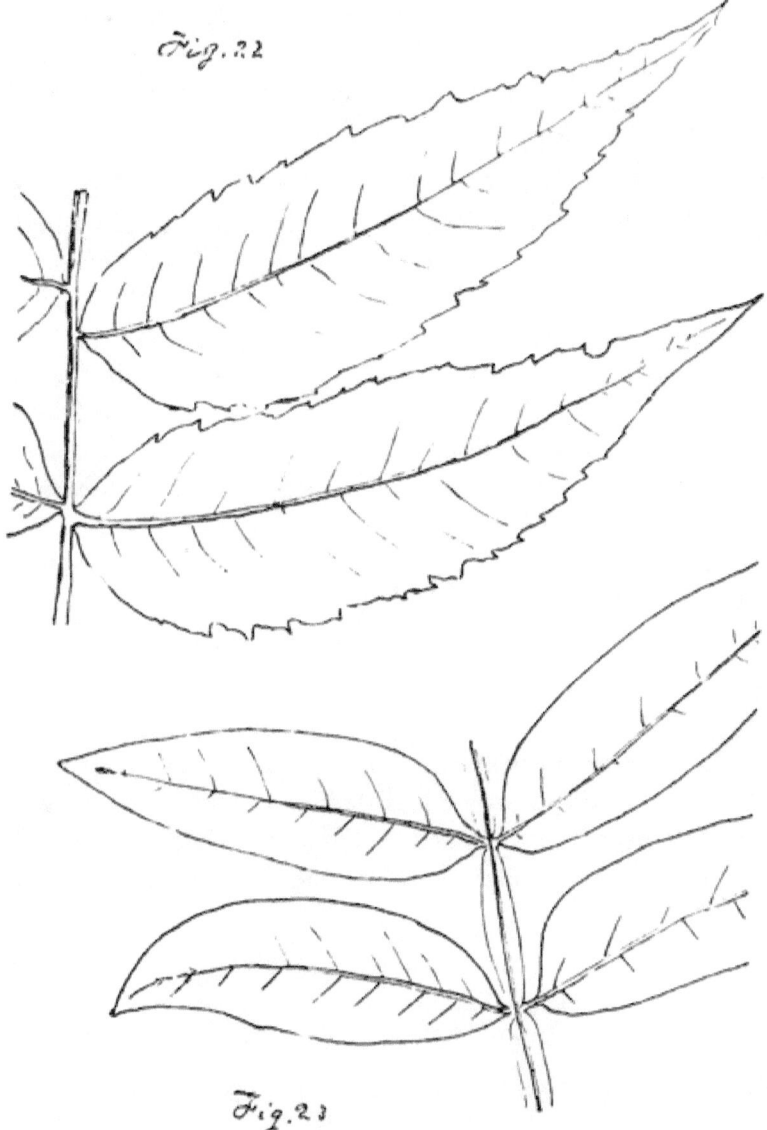

Fig. 22.—Smooth Sumach. (R. glàbra, L.)
Fig. 23.—Dwarf Sumach. (R. copallina, L.)

Sumach (*Anacardiàceæ*)

Fruit, red, with crimson hairs, very sour. *Stone*, smooth. A dry drupe.

Found, very widely distributed in waste and barren places.

A shrub five to fifteen feet high, smooth throughout (excepting in its fruit) with straggling branches, often in extensive clumps and thickets. The bark of this and of other Sumachs is used in tanning. An infusion of the berries makes a pleasant and cooling drink in fevers. Also the berries yield a red dye. In autumn the leaves take a brilliant shade of crimson. The Sumachs are often cultivated; they are easily raised from seed, or they may be propagated from root cuttings.

(2) **Stag-Horn Sumach.** *R. týphina*, L.

Flowers, small, greenish-yellow, crowded in upright, pyramid-shaped, terminal clusters. June.

Leaflets, closely resembling those of the preceding species (the Smooth Sumach), eleven- to thirty-one-toothed, whitish and more or less downy beneath. *Leaf-stem* and branchlets, especially toward their ends, covered with a very dense velvet-like and often crimson-tinged down.

Fruit, rounded, somewhat flattened, covered with a crimson and very acid down. *Stone*, smooth. A dry drupe. September, October.

Found, oftenest in rocky and barren places from New Brunswick and the valley of the St. Lawrence through the Northern States, and southward along the Alleghany Mountains to Central Alabama.

A larger shrub than the Smooth Sumach, sometimes twenty feet high, and often taking the tree form. The straggling, evenly spreading branches, with the leaves

Sumach (Anacardiaceæ)

mostly toward their ends, give a peculiar umbrella-like look. The wood is very soft and brittle, yellow, with the sap-wood white. In spring in the sugar orchards the young shoots, cleared of their pith, serve as "sap quills" for drawing the running sap from the maples. The wood forms a yellow dye, and an infusion of the berries is used as a gargle for sore-throat. The thick down upon the young branches, and their shape, are suggestive of the horns of a stag, whence the name.

Fig. 23.—(3) Dwarf Sumach. Mountain Sumach. *R. copallina, L.*

Flowers, small, greenish, in upright pyramid-shaped, stemless clusters, toward the ends of the branches. July.

Leaflets, nine to twenty-one (oftenest nine to thirteen), one to three inches long, edge entire, base usually rounded and one-sided, upper surface dark and shining. *Leaf-stem*, expanded between the pairs of leaflets into broadly winged margins.

Fruit, rounded, hairy, varying in color in ripening from delicate neutral tints, grays and drabs, to red; acid. *Stone*, smooth. September.

Found, very widely distributed, usually in dry and rocky places.

A shrub three to five feet high, or sometimes, in favorable locations, twenty feet high, oftenest forming clumps or borders along the edge of woods and thickets. Its peculiar winged foliage, and the constantly changing tints of flower, fruit, and leaf, make it the most attractive of the Sumachs, and best worthy of ornamental cultivation. A mass of them set in a corner of the garden or grounds would be constantly attractive.

Sumach (Anacardiaceæ)

Fig. 24.—(4) **Poison Sumach. Poison Dogwood. Poison Elder.** *R. vernix, L.* *(R. venenata, D. C.)*

Flowers, small, green, in long, loose clusters at the bases of the upper leaves. June.

Leaflets, seven to thirteen, edge entire, long oval or egg-shape, smooth and thin, base rounded or pointed. *Leaf-stem*, red throughout, and not winged.

Fruit, about the size of small peas, rounded, smooth, shining, dry. *Stone*, lined. A dry drupe. September.

Found, in swampy land, widely distributed.

A tall shrub (or sometimes a small tree) six to eighteen feet high. It is violently poisonous to the touch, causing, in most persons, a painful eruption; some are poisoned by it without touching it, probably by means of the drifting pollen of its flowers. A recommended application is sugar of lead, applied after the use of saline cathartics, or a thick paste of bicarbonate of soda rubbed into the skin as soon as the eruption appears. It is also claimed that relief and, if used promptly, frequent cure follow the use of belladonna, of apis mellifica, or of arsenicum album, taken in homœopathic doses. But there are wellnigh as many recommended antidotes as there are for the bite of a rattlesnake.

Apart from other differences, the Poison Sumach can be easily and quickly distinguished from all other Sumachs by these signs: It differs from the Smooth Sumach and the Stag-Horn Sumach in having the edge of its leaflets entire; from the Dwarf Sumach, by the absence of the winged stem between its leaflets and by its red leaf-stem.

Sumach (Anacardiàceæ) 75

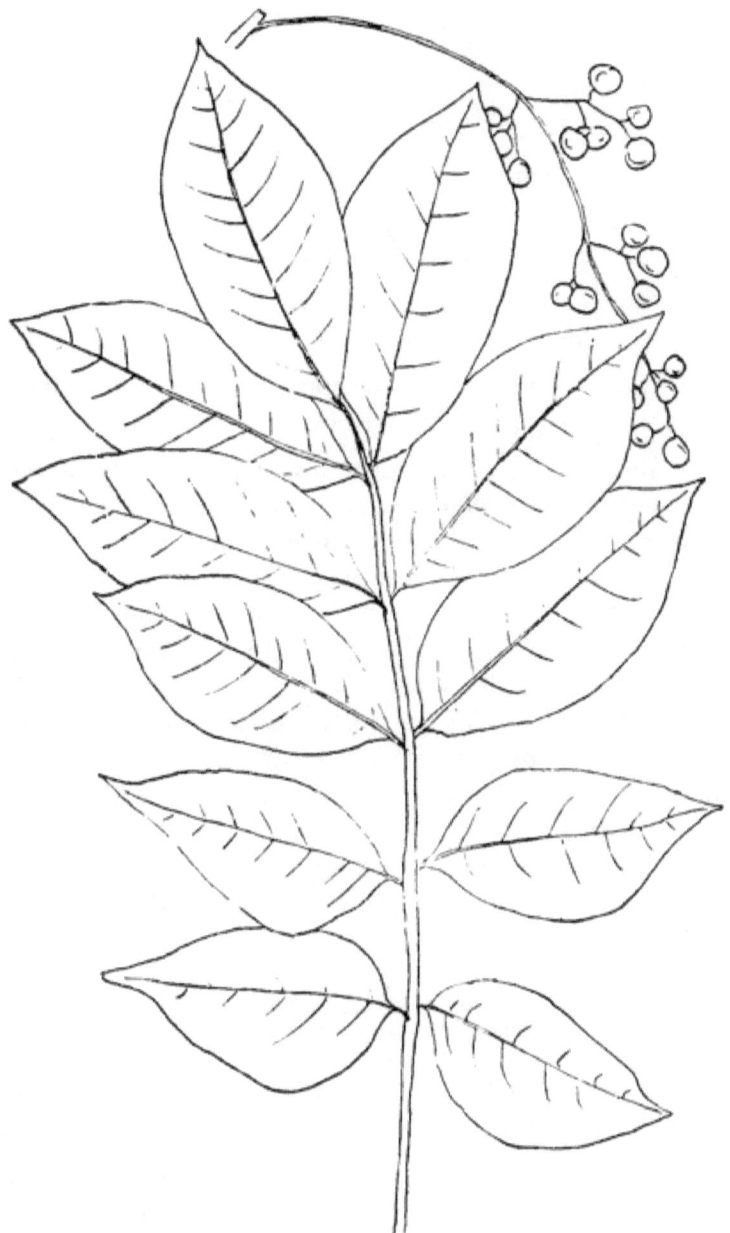

Fig. 24.—Poison Sumach. (R. vérnix, L.)

Sumach (Anacardiàceæ)

Fig. 25.—(5) **Poison Ivy. Poison Oak.** *R. rádicans, L.*
(R. toxicodendron, L.)

Flowers, small, greenish, in loose clusters from the axils of the leaves, the staminate and pistillate forms on different plants.   June.

Leaflets, three, edge entire, or variously sharp-notched, mostly pointed, and somewhat downy beneath.

Fruit, small, rounded, pale brown or whitish, smooth. *Stone,* lined.   September.

Found, widely distributed in open grounds and among trees, along walls and fences.

A shrub that is less poisonous than the Poison Sumach, but more dreaded because the latter is confined to swampy grounds, while the Poison Ivy is found everywhere. It takes all positions; sometimes it is erect (one to three feet high), often it is prostrate and trailing; oftenest, perhaps, it is climbing. In its climbing form it covers the posts of fences, the trunks and branches of trees, stone walls—clinging tenaciously wherever it goes by multitudes of thread-like rootlets, and sometimes reaching a distance of forty or even fifty feet, with a stem from two to five or six inches in diameter. At times it so closely covers its growing support as to smother it. Its poisonous qualities are the same in kind as those of the Poison Sumach.

Fig. 26.—(6) **Sweet Sumach.** *R. aromática, Ait.*
(R. Canadénsis, Marsh.)

Flowers, small, yellowish, in small spikes or heads, unfolding before the leaves.

Leaflets, three, one to three inches long, the end one sometimes three-cleft, edge unequally round-toothed.

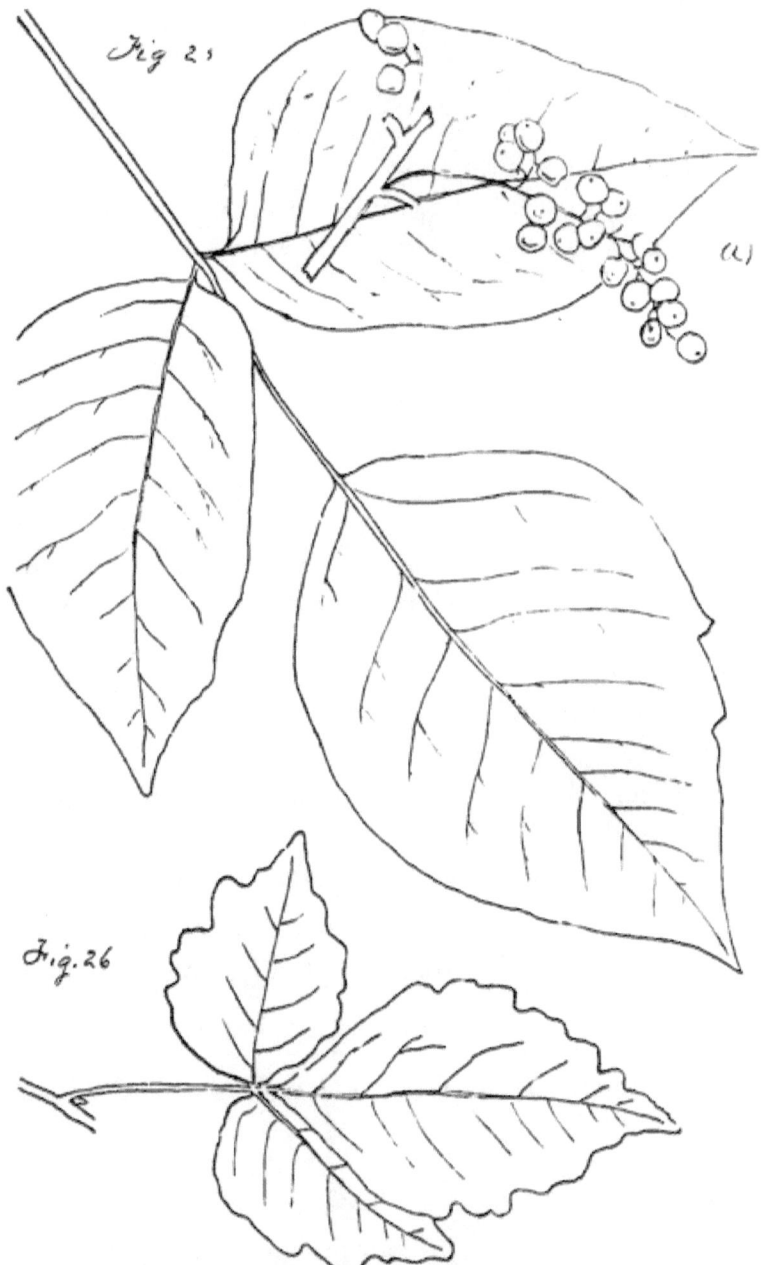

Fig. 25.—Poison Ivy. (R. rádicans, L.) (¹) Fruit.
Fig. 26.—Sweet Sumach. (R. aromática, Ait.)

Fruit, rounded, red, acid.   A dry drupe.

Found, widely distributed north and south on dry open ground, and in thickets.

A straggling shrub, two to six feet high, with leaves of a pleasant, aromatic odor when crushed.

13. Family LEGUMINÒSÆ.   (Pulse Fam.)

Genus AMÓRPHA, L.   (False Indigo, etc.)

From a Greek word meaning "without form," because of the absence of a part of its petals.

Fig. 27.—False Indigo.   *A. fruticòsa, L.*

Flowers, irregular, violet or purple, crowded in clustered terminal spikes.   *Petal*, one.   *Stamens*, ten, united at the base.   *Sepals*, five.   *Seed-case*, one, one-celled, free, two-seeded, longer than the calyx.   May, June.

Leaves, compound, alternate, three to five inches long.   *Leaflets*, fifteen to seventeen, about one inch long, edge entire, marked with small dots.

Fruit, small, two-seeded.   A pod.

Found, from Southern Pennsylvania southward, and far westward.

A shrub six to sixteen feet high.

Lead-Plant.   *A. canéscens, Nutt.*

This species differs from the preceding chiefly in these items:

Flowers, bright blue.

Leaflets, thirty-one to fifty-one, small (one and a half inches or less), crowded.

Fruit, one-seeded.

Found, westward.

A pretty shrub, two to four feet high, taking its name from a supposed liking for localities containing lead-ore.

Pulse (Leguminosæ) 79

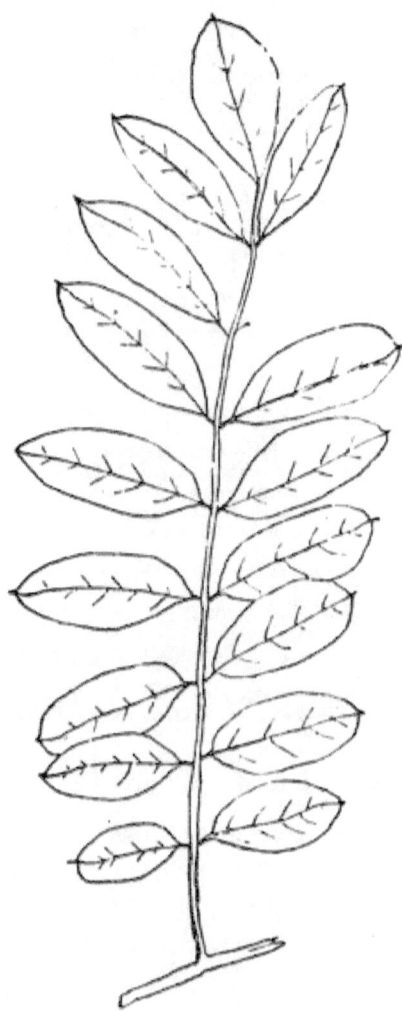

Fig. 27.—False Indigo. (A. fructicòsa, L.)

14. Family ROSÀCEÆ. (Rose Fam.)

Flowers, regular. *Petals*, five, not united, inserted with the stamens on the edge of a disk that lines the tube of the calyx. *Sepals*, five, united toward the base, often accompanied outside by a row of small, leaf-like bracts. *Stamens*, numerous [or in Spiræa (2) sometimes as few as ten] inserted as above. *Seed-case*, one to many, free from the calyx excepting in Pyrus (6), Cratægus (7), and Amelanchior (8), and in the Genus Rosa (5), where the many pistils are imbedded in the inner surface of the more or less rounded calyx-tube.

Leaves, usually simple [compound in Rosa (5) and in Rubus (4) excepting in one species], alternate, usually with leaf-like bracts (stipules) at the base of the leaf-stem.

Guide to the Genera.

(*a*) Seed-case, one to many, free, and not (as in Rosa) covered in ripening by the calyx.
    (*b*) Seed-case, one. Leaves, simple. Fruit, a drupe. (1) Prùnus (Plum, Cherry).
    (*b*) Seed-cases, mostly five, one-celled, two- to several-seeded. Fruit, a follicle.
        (*c*) Leaves, simple. (2) Spiræa (Meadow-Sweet, etc.).
        (*c*) " " lobed. (3) Physocárpus (Nine-Bark).
    (*b*) Seed-cases, numerous, crowded on a lengthened, spongy receptacle, becoming fleshy in fruit. Leaves compound (except in Flowering Raspberry). Fruit, crowded drupelets. (4) Rùbus (Blackberry, etc.).
(*a*) Seed-case, one to many, adherent to the calyx tube, or (in Rosa) covered in ripening by the calyx.
    (2) Seed-cases, many, becoming bony nutlets enclosed in the rounded, fleshy calyx-tube, and appearing like a small apple. Leaves, compound. Fruit, clustered akenes, but apparently a pome. (5) Rosa (Rose).
    (2) Seed-case, one, imbedded in the fleshy calyx tube. Leaves, simple. Fruit, a pome. (6) Pyrus (Chokeberry, etc.), (7) Cratègus (Thorn, Haw), (8) Amelánchior (Juneberry).

(1) Genus Prùnus, Tourn. (Plum, Cherry.)

Flowers, white, in clusters, excepting in the third species (sloe), with or preceding the leaves, excepting in the fourth species (Choke-Cherry). *Petals*, five, much spreading. *Sepals*, five. *Stamens*, fifteen to twenty. *Seed-case*, one, free from the calyx, with two young seeds, only one of which usually ripens.

Leaves, simple, alternate, toothed.

Fruit, fleshy, with a bony stone.

Rose (Rosaceæ)

Fig. 28.—Wild Plum. Canada Plum. Horse Plum.
P. Americana, Marsh.

Flowers, in simple clusters of three to four blossoms, preceding the leaves.

Leaves, two to three inches long, oval to reverse egg-shape; base pointed or rounded, somewhat downy on the veins and in their angles. Bark of the main stem dark, reddish-green, or bronze-green.

Fruit, one half to two thirds inches in diameter, yellow, orange, or red, with a thick, acid skin, and a pleasant flavor. *Stone*, slightly flattened, with both edges winged and sharp.

Found, from Canada southward to Florida, and westward, and often in cultivation.

A bush (or sometimes a small tree) eight to twenty feet high, with hard, reddish wood. In cultivation it furnishes an excellent stock on which to graft the domestic plums.

Dwarf Cherry. Sand Cherry. *P. pumila, L.*

Flowers, two to four, together.

Leaves, narrowly reverse egg-shape, tapering to the base, slightly toothed toward the apex, pale beneath.

Fruit, slightly lengthened, nearly black when ripe, usually sour and puckery. *Stone*, lengthened, without margin, the size of a large pea.

Found, from Canada to Virginia, and westward.

A drooping and trailing shrub, six inches to six feet high.

Fig. 29.—Beach Plum. *P. maritima*, Wang.

Flowers, white, two to five in each cluster, appearing before the leaves. April, May.

Leaf, one to three inches long, edge very finely toothed, outline mostly oval, light green, soft, downy beneath, especially when young, strongly net-veined. *Leaf-stem*, with two small, wart-like dots. *Bark*, very dark.

Fruit, one half to one inch in diameter, round or oval, purple or crimson. *Stone*, much swollen, sharp on one edge, on the opposite side rounded and finely grooved; edible. Ripe in August and September.

Found, on and near the sea-beach from Massachusetts to Virginia.

A straggling, much-branching bush, two to five feet high. The farther it grows from the beach, the thinner and smoother its leaves are likely to be, and its plums smaller. Its fruit is much sought in autumn for preserving. "Beach-plumming" along the coast equals in interest "chestnutting" and "huckleberrying" inland.

Prunus Alleghaniénsis. *Porter.*

Leaves, long oval to lanceolate.

Fruit, very dark purple, less than one half inch in diameter. *Stone*, with a broad flat ridge on one side, and a shallow groove on the other.

Found, on the bluffs of the Alleghany Mountains in Pennsylvania.

A straggling shrub, or sometimes a small tree, three to fifteen feet high, seldom thorny.

Rose (Rosàceæ)

Fig. 28.—Wild Plum. (P. Americàna, Marsh.) (a) Fruit.
Fig. 29.—Beach Plum. (P. maritima, Wang.) (b) Fruit.

Rose (Rosàceæ)

Fig. 30.—Sloe. Black Thorn. [*P. spinòsa. L.*]

Flowers, white, usually solitary. *Flower-stems*, smooth.

Leaves, edge sharply-toothed or double-toothed, reverse egg-shape to egg-shape, downy beneath, becoming smooth.

Fruit, small, rounded, black. *Stone*, swollen, with one edge sharp.

Found, in waste places from New England to Pennsylvania, and New Jersey. Introduced from Europe.

A thorny shrub, twelve to fifteen feet high.

Fig. 31.—Choke-Cherry. *P. Virginiàna, L.*

Flowers, white, with short stems, set in a long, cylinder-shaped cluster at the ends of leafy branchlets, appearing after the leaves. *Petals*, rounded. May.

Leaves, two to three inches long, oval to reverse egg-shape, thin, base variable, edge finely and sharply toothed. *Leaf-stem*, usually marked with two to four wart-like dots. *Bark*, light gray or greenish on the young shoots, becoming dark gray after the first year.

Fruit, about one quarter inch in diameter, very abundant, red, becoming very dark in ripening, exceedingly astringent (puckery), but when thoroughly ripe not unpalatable. *Stone*, rounded, smooth, without margin. July, August.

Found, widely distributed in woods and hedges from Georgia westward and northward. Common, especially northward.

A shrub (or sometimes a small tree) five to twenty feet high.

Fig. 30.—Sloe. [P. spinòsa, L.]
Fig. 31.—Choke-Cherry. (P. Virginiàna, L.) (a) Fruit.

Rose (Rosàceæ)

(2) Genus SPIRÆA, L. (Meadow-Sweet, etc.)

Flowers, white to rose-color, crowded in rounded or pyramid-shaped or steeple-shaped clusters. *Petals*, five, reverse egg-shape. *Stamens*, ten to fifty. *Seed-cases*, mostly five, distinct, one-celled, several-seeded.

Leaves, simple, alternate, toothed.

Fruit, a dry, simple case (usually in clusters of five), with one cell and several long, slim seeds; a follicle, or a cluster of follicles.

Fig. 32.—Meadow-Sweet. *S. salicifolia, L.*

Flowers, small, white or tinged with rose, crowded in rounded and pyramid-shaped terminal clusters. *Seed-cases*, five, smooth. July, August.

Leaves, one and one half to three inches long, smooth or nearly so, oval to reverse egg-shape, singly or doubly sharp-toothed, base pointed or rounded. *Apex*, pointed.

Fruit, as above.

Found, from Georgia northward and westward, most abundantly in low grounds.

A shrub three to four feet high, erect, with polished copper-colored or purplish brittle stem, ornamental in cultivation.

Fig. 33.—Birch-Leaved Spiræa. *S. corymbòsa, Raf.*

This species differs chiefly in the following items:

Flowers, in large, flat clusters. *Seed-cases*, three to five.

Leaves, broad oval or ovate, toothed only toward the apex.

Found, in the mountains of Pennsylvania and New Jersey, southward to Georgia, and westward to Kentucky and Missouri.

A shrub one to two feet high.

Rose (Rosaceæ)

Fig. 32.—Meadow-Sweet. (S. salicifòlia, L.)
Fig. 33.—Birch-Leaved Spiræa. (S. corymbòsa, Raf.)

Fig. 34.—**Hardhack. Steeple-Bush.** *S. tomentosa, L.*

Flowers, small, rose-colored or rarely white, crowded in steeple-shaped, terminal clusters. *Seed-cases*, five, woolly. July, August.

Leaves, crowded, egg-shape or oblong, toothed, very white-woolly beneath. *New shoots*, covered with a rusty down. *Old stems*, smooth, and of a bronze color.

Fruit, as above.

Found, in low ground from Georgia northward and westward.

A small shrub, two to five feet high, with hard, brittle stalks, that call for troublesome "hacking" on the part of the haymakers, whence one of its names. It is ornamental, and is often cultivated for its pretty, steeple-like clusters of late-blooming, rosy flowers.

(3) Genus PHYSOCARPUS, Maxim. (Nine-Bark.)

From two Greek words meaning "bladder" and "nut."

Fig. 35.—**Nine-Bark.** *P. opulifolius (L.) Maxim.*

Flowers, small, white, often purple-tinged, in close, rounded clusters two and one half inches in diameter, each flower with a thread-like, downy stem. *Petals*, five. *Stamens*, thirty to forty. *Seed-cases*, one to five, inflated. *Young seeds*, two to four. June.

Leaves, one to two and one half inches long, three-lobed, with the lobes sharply toothed, base somewhat heart-shaped or pointed. *Bark*, gray, loose, and flaking off in thin scales.

Fruit, conspicuous, a smooth, simple case, inflated and purplish, with one cell and two ripened seeds, usually in clusters of three to five. *Seeds*, rounded, smooth, and shining. A follicle or cluster of follicles.

Fig. 34.—Hardhack. (S. tomentòsa, L.)
Fig. 35.—Nine-Bark. (P. opulifòlius L., Maxim.)

Rose (Rosàceæ)

Found, oftenest on the banks of streams from Canada southward and westward, widely distributed, but rather rare in its wild state.

A beautiful shrub, three to five feet high, often and easily cultivated.

(4) Genus RUBUS, Tourn. (Blackberry, etc.)

From a word meaning "red."

Flowers, white (excepting in the first species, Purple-Flowering Raspberry). *Petals*, five. *Sepals*, five, partly united, spreading. *Stamens*, numerous. *Seed-cases*, many, each with two young seeds, only one of which ripens, crowded on a lengthened receptacle.

Leaves, compound (excepting in Purple-Flowering Raspberry). *Stems*, often armed with prickles.

Fruit, a pulpy edible "berry" so called, formed by the ripened seed-cases. A mass of small drupes.

Fig. 36.—Purple-Flowering Raspberry. *R. odoràtus, L.*

Flowers, one to two inches across, showy, purple to rose color. *Petals*, rounded in terminal clusters. *Stamens*, one hundred to two hundred, whitish. *Calyx*, flower-stems, and branchlets, covered with sticky hairs. June, July.

Leaves, four to eight inches long, simple, three- to five-lobed, the middle lobe longest, all pointed and with their edges fine-toothed, somewhat hairy, without prickles.

Fruit, of but slight value, broad and flat, sometimes an inch across, separating from the receptacle when ripe, red, sweet when ripe. August.

Fig. 36.—Purple-Flowering Raspberry. R. odorátus, L.

Found, from Georgia northward and westward, often in rocky places, and on the borders of dry woods.

A straggling shrub, three to five feet high. Its rose-like blossoms and its late summer flowering make it worthy of cultivation. It requires shade.

Fig. 37.—Wild Red Raspberry. *R. strigosus*, Michx.

Flowers, small, white. *Petals*, erect, as long as the sepals. May.

Leaflets, three to five, the side ones without stems, whitish-downy beneath. *Stems*, thickly set with stiff bristles that are usually straight, but sometimes hooked.

Fruit, half round, red, when ripe falling from the lengthened receptacle, sweet, and very pleasant to the taste. June, August.

Found, especially along roadsides and in neglected fields, from Labrador to New Jersey, and westward and southward along the mountains to North Carolina.

A free-growing shrub, three to six feet high, ranking with the blackberries and huckleberries as a liberal and welcome fruit-giver for country homes. The supplies for the city markets are mostly from cultivated varieties.

Fig. 38.—Blackcap. Black Raspberry. Thimbleberry.
R. occidentalis, L.

This species differs from the preceding chiefly in the following items:

Flowers, with petals shorter than the sepals.

Leaflets, usually three, rarely five, the side ones sometimes with short stems.

Fruit, black, rarely whitish.

Rose (Rosàceæ)

Fig 37.—Red Raspberry. (R. strigòsus, Michx.)

Rose (Rosàceæ)

The shrub spreads by help of long branches which curve over and down until their tips touch the ground, and root, so forming new centres of tangled growth.

High Blackberry. *R. villòsus, Ait.*

Flowers, numerous, in clusters of about twenty blossoms. *Petals*, spreading, reverse egg-shape, much longer than the narrow, pointed sepals.

Leaflets, three (or sometimes five), usually with prickly stems, not whitish-downy beneath. *Leaves* and branchlets hairy and glandular. *Stems*, furrowed and ridged, and armed with stout curved prickles.

Fruit, oblong, black, not separating when ripe from the lengthened receptacle. August, September.

Found, oftenest along roadsides and in thickets. Common.

A scraggly, thorny bush, three to six feet high, with a very pleasant-flavored fruit. A tea from the steeped root is a home remedy for summer complaint.

Rùbus villòsus, var. frondòsus, Torr.

This variety has about ten flowers in a cluster, with petals more rounded than the last, is smoother, and has fewer drupelets in the more acid fruit. It is found with the type at the North.

Sand Blackberry. *R. cuneifòlius, Pursh.*

Flowers, white (sometimes with a rose tint). *Petals*, large, three times as long as the sepals, in two- to four-blossomed clusters. May, June.

Leaflets, three (sometimes five), stemless, somewhat wedge-shape and reverse egg-shape, whitish-downy beneath, edge entire toward the base. *Leaf-stems*, downy, often prickly, young branches downy beneath. *Stems*, round, and armed with stout, re-curved prickles.

Rose (Rosaceæ)

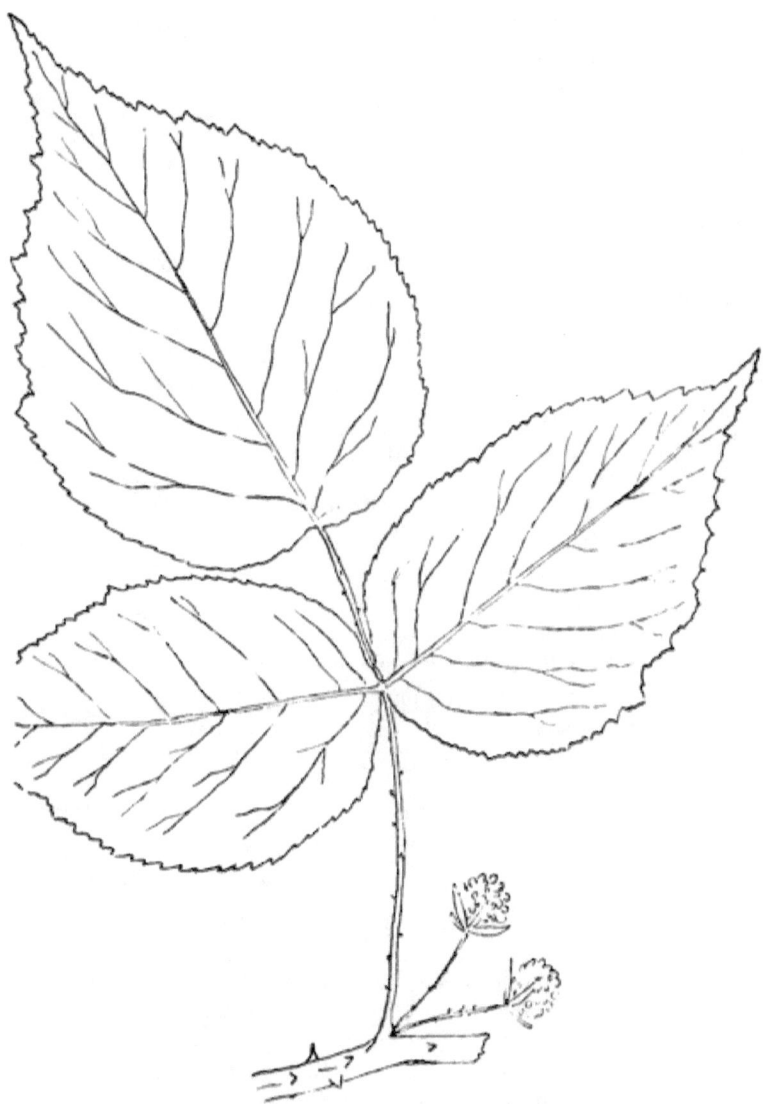

Fig. 38.—Blackcap. (R. occidentális, L.)

Rose (Rosàceæ)

Fruit, black, well-flavored. July, August.

Found, in sandy woods of southern New York and Pennsylvania, southward and westward.

A shrub two to three feet high.

(5) Genus Rósa, Tourn. (Rose.)

Flowers, with five reverse egg-shape or reverse heart-shape petals. *Calyx-tube*, fleshy, contracted at the throat, urn-shaped. *Stamens*, many. *Pistils*, many, embedded in the inner surface of the calyx-tube.

Leaves, compound (odd-feathered), alternate, edge of leaflets toothed, lower edges of the leaf-stem with prominent wings (stipules).

Fruit, a more or less reddish or greenish ball ("hip") enclosing the many dry one-seeded seed-cases. A covered cluster of akenes.

"If Jove would give the leafy bowers
 A queen for all their world of flowers,
 The rose would be the choice of Jove,
 And blush, the queen of every grove."—TH. MOORE.

"The rose doth deserve the chiefest and most principall place among all flowers whatsoever, . . . for his beautie, his vertues, and his flagrant and odoriferous smell.—*Gérard's Herball*, London, 1597.

"The rose is the honor and beautie of flowres,
 The rose is the care and the love of the Spring,
 The rose is the pleasure of the 'avenly powers:
 The boy of faire *Venus, Cythere's* darling,
 Doth wrap his head round with garlands of rose,
 When to the daunces of the Graces he goes."—
    Gérard's Herball, London, 1597.

"But there are many kinds of Roses differing either in the bignesse of the flowers, or the plant itself, roughnes or smoothnes, or in the multitude of the flowers, or in the fewnesse, or else in color and smell."—*Gérard's Herball.* London, 1597.

Shining Rose. *R. lucida, Ehrh.*

Flowers, pale red, generally in one to three pairs. *Petals*, large, slightly two-lobed. *Sepals*, spreading after flowering, presently falling away, the outer ones often with two small lobes; the sepals and the rounded receptacle usually hairy. June, July.

Leaves, smooth, and often shining above. *Leaf-stem*, usually somewhat hairy, and with spines between the "wings." *Leaflets*, mostly seven, acute or blunt, coarse-toothed, stemless except the end one. *Stems*, mostly greenish. *Spines*, straight or sometimes hooked, becoming stout. *Prickles*, scattered.

Fruit, rounded, red, small, depressed, with the fruit-stem glandular-hairy.

Found widely distributed in woods and thickets, and waste grounds.

A shrub usually one to three feet high.

Low Rose. *R. humilis, Marsh.*

This species is quite variable. It differs from the last in the following items:

Outer Sepals, always more or less lobed.
Leaflets, usually thinner and paler.
Stipules, usually narrow.
Spines, usually straight and slender.
Found, mostly in dry soil from Maine to Georgia, and westward.

Wild Rose. *R. nitida, Willd.*

This species differs from *R. lucida* chiefly in the following items:

Flowers, solitary (rarely in twos or threes). *Petals,* red. *Sepals,* entire. June.

Leaflets, usually narrow and pointed at each end, nearly stemless excepting the end one. *Stems,* reddened by their dense covering of straight and slender prickles.

Fruit, scarlet.

Found, in swampy ground from Newfoundland to New England and New York.

A shrub one to two feet high.

Carolina Rose. Swamp Rose. *R. Carolina, L.*

Flowers, in leafy clusters of three to seven blossoms, large, red to white. *Petals,* slightly two-lobed. *Sepals,* spreading, and falling away after flowering.

Leaflets, five to nine (mostly seven), sharply and often doubly fine-toothed, dull green, not shining above, rather variable in shape. *Prickles,* mostly two at the base of each leaf-stem.

Fruit, dark red, depressed and rounded.

Found, along streams and in swamps, in damp woods and thickets from Nova Scotia to Florida, and westward.

A bushy shrub four to eight feet high with reddish stalks. A very variable species.

Fig. 39.—Bland Rose. *R. blanda, Ait.*

Flowers, usually large, clustered or solitary. *Petals,* reddish, with a small notch at the end. *Sepals,* entire, shorter than the petals, drawing together after flow-

Rose (Rosàceæ)

Fig. 39.—Bland Rose. (R. blánda, Ait.)

ering, and not falling off. *Bracts*, under the blossom large and downy. June.

Leaflets, five to seven, toothed, wedge-shaped at the base, with short stems, not shining above. *Leaf-stem*, unarmed. *Stems*, with a reddish bark. *Prickles*, none, or few, scattered and straight.

Fruit, rounded.

Found, among rocks and on open hills around the Great Lakes, and from Newfoundland to Central New York.

A shrub two to three feet high.

Sweet Brier. Eglantine. [*R. rubiginosa*, L.]

Flowers, light red, mostly solitary, on short, bristly stems, fragrant. *Sepals*, hairy, with slashed or toothed edge, not falling off in ripening.

Leaflets, five to seven, one half to two thirds inches long, usually thickly covered beneath with resinous glands, very fragrant when crushed. *Leaf-stem*, hairy. *Prickles*, mostly strong and recurved.

Fruit, orange-red, oblong to reverse egg-shape.

Found, in waste fields and along roadsides from South Carolina and Tennessee northward. Introduced from Europe.

A stout shrub four to eight feet high.

(6) Genus PYRUS, L. (Chokeberry, etc.)

Fig. 40.—**Chokeberry.** *P. arbutifolia*, *L. f.*

Flowers, white or reddish, in clusters, usually of about twelve blossoms. *Petals*, five, roundish. *Calyx*, urn-shaped. *Styles*, united toward the base. Calyx and flower-stem downy when young. May, June.

Fig. 40.—Chokeberry. (P. arbutifòlia, L. f.)
Fig. 41.—Dogberry. P. nigra (Marsh), Sargent.

Leaves, simple, fine-toothed, downy beneath when young, marked with small reddish warts along the midvein above, oval to reverse egg-shape. *Apex*, pointed or blunt.

Fruit, dark red or purple, about the size of a small currant, rounded or pear-shaped, with five cells and ten seeds, puckery. A berry-like pome.

Found, in damp ground, often forming extensive thickets, common from Nova Scotia to Florida, and westward.

A vigorous shrub, five to eight feet high.

Fig. 41.—**Dogberry.** *P. nigra (Marsh), Sargent. (P. arbutifolia var. melanocárpa, Hook.)*

This variety differs from the preceding chiefly in these items:

Sepals, Flower-stems, and *Leaves*, all smooth or nearly so.

Fruit, larger, black, less puckery often mistaken by the children for large huckleberries; ripening earlier.

Found, often in dry as well as wet ground.

A shrub one to four feet high.

FROM NOTE BOOK:
I.—"What do you call that, boys?"
Two Boys.—"Dogberry. It ain't good to eat!"
I.—"It is n't poisonous, is it?"
Two Boys.—Yes, 't is.

Where the boys found that name I do not know, nor do I know their reasons for thinking the berry poisonous. They may have experimented, or, as men sometimes do in greater matters, they may simply have repeated a slanderous tradition. I remember that as a boy I often found the little shrub growing among the huckleberry bushes, and was afraid of mistaking its berries for the safe huckleberries. Yet I never heard of any case of poisoning from them. I imagine that the boys were right in considering the berry not desirable for food, but I doubt their estimate of its poisonous qualities.

(7) Genus CRATÆGUS. (Thorn. Haw.)

From a Greek word meaning "strength," because of the firmness of the wood.

Flowers, white, rarely rose color, in clusters. *Petals*, five, rounded. *Stamens*, many. *Calyx-tube*, urn-shaped. *Styles*, one to five. *Seed-cases*, one to five.

Leaves, simple, toothed, often with deep clefts, almost forming small lobes. *Stems*, armed with thorns.

Fruit, fleshy, with one to five stones, crowned by the persistent sepals. A drupe.

Sir John Mandeville visited Palestine in the 14th century. There he saw a crown which was said to be the Saviour's "crown of thorns." He comments concerning our Lord and the crown: "In that nyghte that He was taken, He was yled into a gardyn; and there He was first examyned righte scharply; and there the Jewes scorned Hym, and maden Hym a crowne of the braunches of Albespyne, that is White Thorn, that grew in the same gardyn, and setten yt on His head, so faste and so sore, that the blood ran down be many places of Hys visage, and of Hys necke, and of Hys schulders. And therefore hath the White Thorn many vertues; for he that berethe a braunche on him thereof, no thondre, ne no maner of tempest may dere him; ne in the hows that yt is inne may non evylle gost entre."

"'T is commonly say'd, in Germany, that the Witches doe meet in the night before the first day of May, upon an high mountain called the Blocks-berg; and the common people doe the night before ye said day fetch a certain Thorn, and stick it at their house-door, believing the witches can then doe them no harm."—AUBREY.

Fig. 42.—White Thorn. Scarlet-Fruited Thorn. Red Haw.
C. coccinea, L.

Flowers, about two thirds of an inch across, white (often with a rosy tinge), twelve or so in a bunch, with a strong and rather disagreeable odor. May.

Leaves, with five to nine deep cuts, almost forming small lobes, usually one and a half to two and a half inches long, but variable in size even on the same tree, thin, smooth, shining. *Base*, usually slightly pointed, but often blunt or slightly heart-shaped. *Leaf-stem*, slender (in *var. macracántha*, Dudley, stout), and often with small wart-like glands. *Branchlets*, usually greenish, or whitish as though washed with silver. *Thorns*, one to two inches long, stout, often whitish, usually slightly curved.

Fruit, nearly half an inch in diameter, rounded or egg-shape; bright red or purple, with thin pulp. Somewhat edible. September.

Found, through the Atlantic forests southward to Northern Florida and Eastern Texas.

A shrub (or often a low tree) ten to twenty feet high, with crooked and spreading branches; very common in the North, rare in the South.

Var. móllis T. and G., with its leaves downy, at least on the under side, and with its red fruit large and downy, is found from Central Michigan southward and westward.

Rose (Rosaceæ)

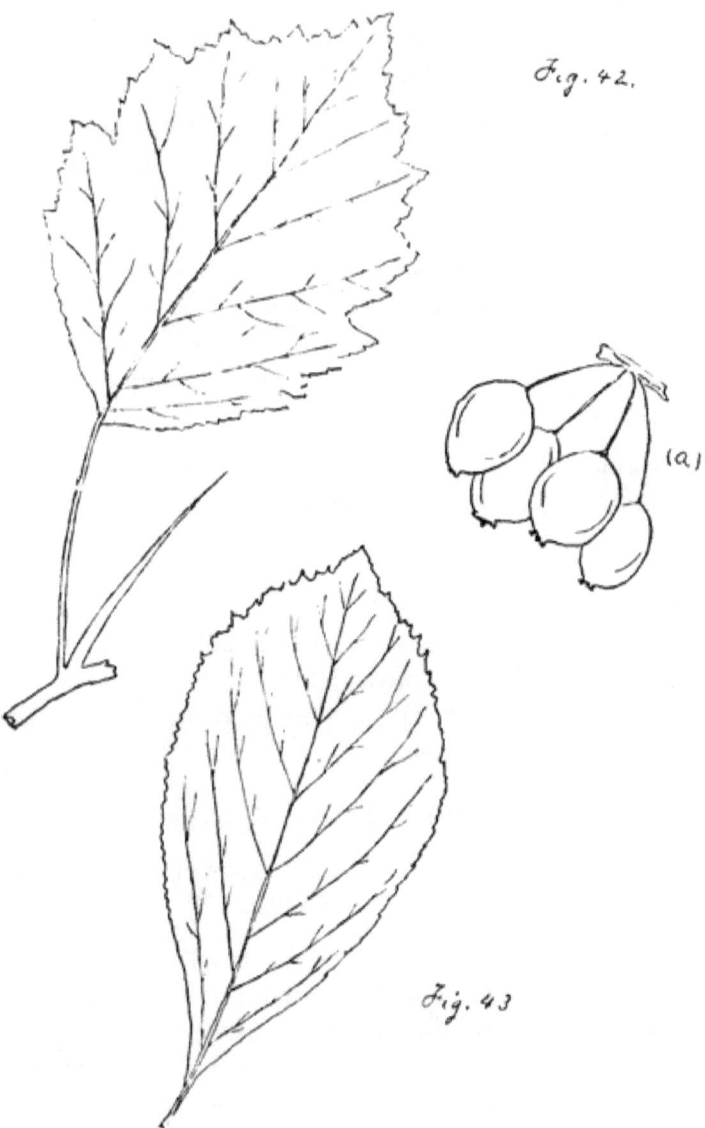

Fig. 42.—White Thorn. (C. coccinea, L.) (a) Fruit.
Fig. 43.—Black Thorn. (C. tomentòsa, L.)

Fig. 43.—**Black Thorn. Pear Thorn.** *C. tomentosa*, L.

Flowers, often one inch across, white, eight to twelve in a cluster, fragrant. May, June.

Leaves, variable, sometimes with quite deep and sharp cuts, almost forming small lobes, about three to five inches long, oval to reverse egg-shape, tapering in a hollow curve, and along the sides of the leaf-stem to a point; under surface downy, at least when young, permanently downy on the veins. *Leaf-stem*, bordered by the leaf, to its base. *Thorns*, one to two inches long. *Bark* of trunk smooth and gray, new twigs light greenish-brown.

Fruit, about one half inch in diameter, round or pear-shaped, orange-red or crimson; edible. October.

Found, through the Atlantic forests to Western Florida, and far westward; common.

A thickly branching shrub (or small tree) eight to twenty feet high, the most widely distributed of the American Thorns. It varies greatly in size and in the style of its fruit and leaves.

Fig. 44.—**Cockspur Thorn.** *C. crus-galli*, L.

Flowers, white, fragrant, in clusters of about fifteen blossoms on very short side branchlets. June.

Leaves, sharply toothed toward the apex, entire below, one to two and one half inches long, thick, very smooth, and shining above, reverse egg-shape, or reverse lance-shape to somewhat oval. *Apex*, usually rounded, sometimes pointed. *Base*, tapering to a point, quite variable. *Leaf-stem*, short. *Thorns*, two to three inches long, rather slender, and straight.

Rose (Rosàceæ)

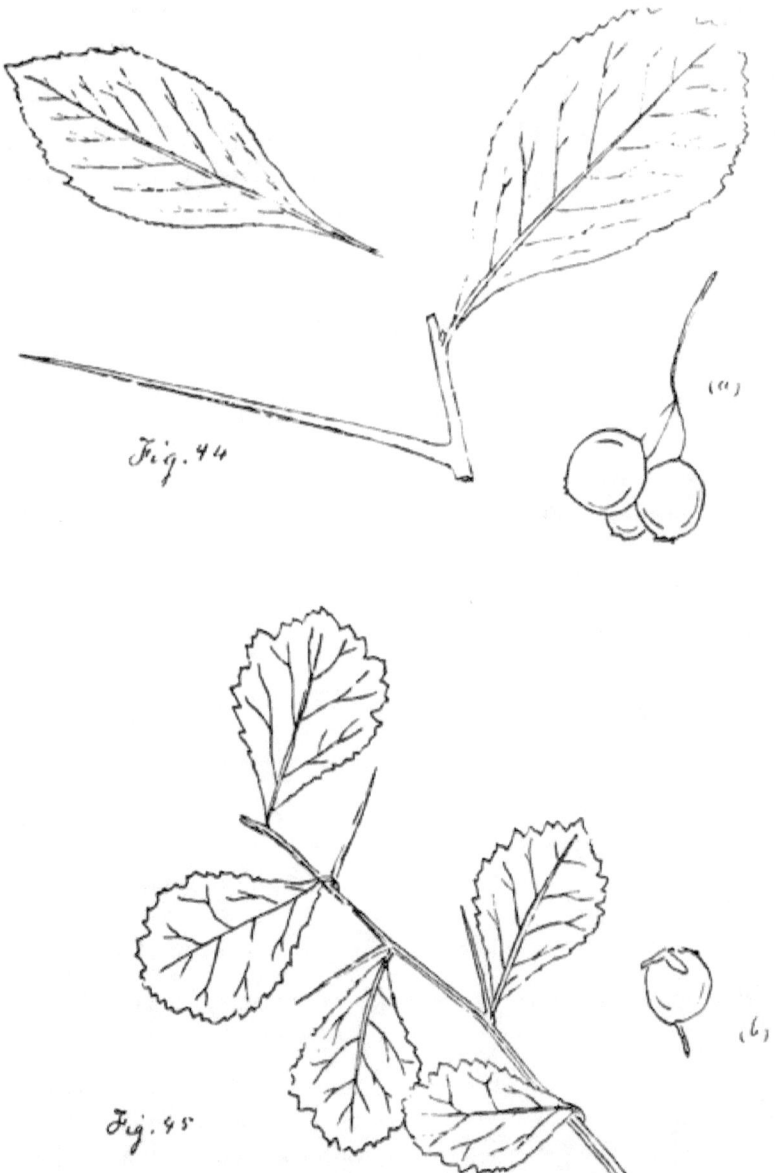

Fig. 44.—Cockspur Thorn. (C. crus-gálli, L.) (*a*) Fruit.
Fig. 45.—Dwarf Thorn. (C. uniflòra, Münch.) (*b*) Fruit.

Fruit, about one third inch in diameter, pear-shape or round, red, remaining during the winter.

Found, along the St. Lawrence and westward, and from Vermont southward and westward; not common.

A thick-branching shrub (or small tree) ten to twenty feet high. It is the best species of thorn for hedges.

Fig. 45.—Dwarf Thorn.   *C. uniflora, Munch.   C. parvifolia, Ait.*

Flowers, solitary, or two or three together, appearing with the leaves. *Sepals*, downy, with edges slashed or toothed, as long as the petals. *Styles*, five. *Flower-stems*, very short, downy.   April, May.

Leaves, thick, downy when young, becoming smooth and shining above, one half to one and one half inches long, nearly stemless. *Branchlets*, downy. *Thorns*, straight and slender.

Fruit, round or pear-shape, yellowish, about one half inch in diameter; edible.

Found, in sandy soil, New Jersey and southward.

A scraggy shrub, three to six feet high.

The English Hawthorn *(C. oxyacántha, L.)* is often found in cultivation; rarely naturalized and growing wild.

(8) Genus AMELÁNCHIER, Medik.   (June-berry.)

Fig. 46.—June-berry. Shad-bush. May Cherry. Service Tree.
A. Canadénsis (L.), Medik.

Flowers, large, white, in long, loose clusters at the ends of the branchlets, appearing before the leaves. *Petals*, lengthened. *Sepals*, downy within. *Stamens*, numerous, and short. *Styles*, five, united below.

Calycanthus (Calycanthàceæ)

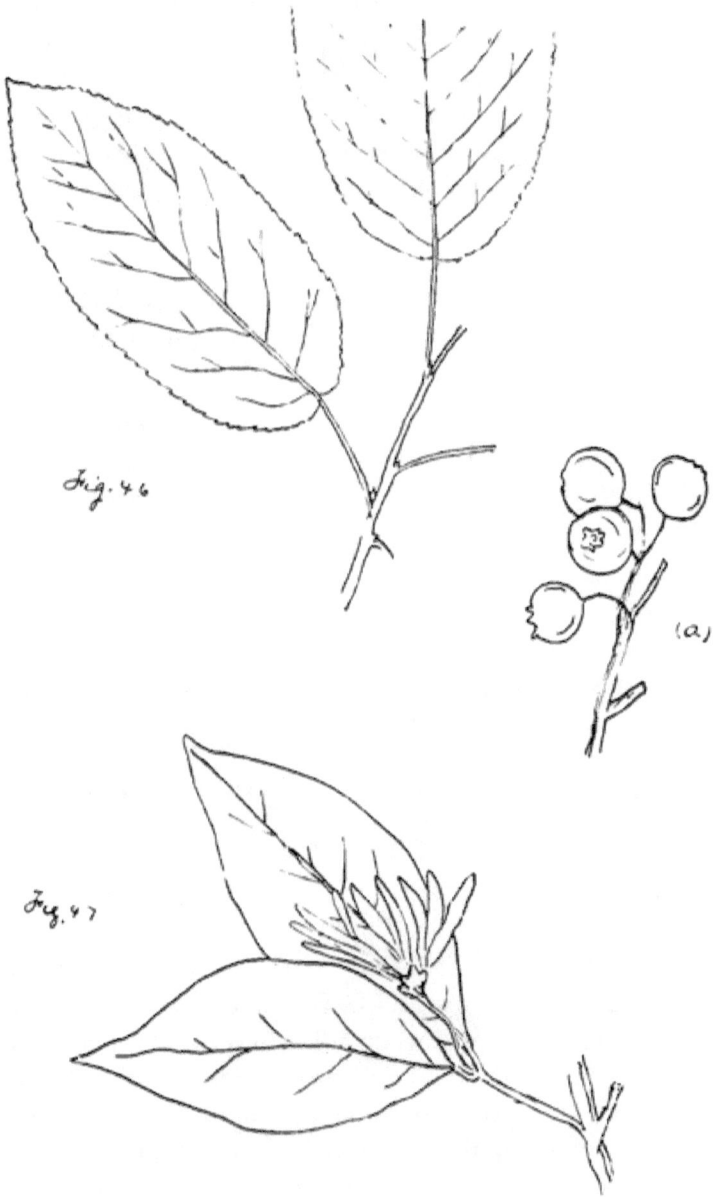

Fig. 46.—June-berry. A. Canadensis (L.), Medik. (a) Fruit.
Fig. 47.—Sweet-scented Shrub. (C. nànus, Loisel.)

Seed-case, five-celled, but becoming ten-celled by false partitions, with ten young seeds, only a part of which sometimes ripen.

Leaves, variable, long egg-shape to reverse egg-shape. *Base*, slightly heart-shaped or rounded. *Apex*, sometimes bristle-pointed, usually two to three inches long, somewhat downy when young, afterward very smooth above and below. *Bark*, of branches and twigs usually purplish-brown and very smooth.

Fruit, berry-like, round, purplish, sweet, and edible. A pome. June, August.

Found, in woods and along streams, common in the North, rare in the South.

A shrub (or sometimes tree), five to thirty feet high.

A. spicàta (Lam.) Dec. (Var. oblongifòlia, Torr. and G.), A. oligocárpa (Michx.) Roem., and *A. alnifòlia, Nutt.*, are smaller forms found northward.

The name "shad-bush" is given because the shrub blossoms about the time the shad "run."

15. Family CALYCANTHÀCEÆ. (Calycanthus Fam.)

Genus CALYCÁNTHUS, L.

Fig. 47.—Sweet-scented Shrub. Carolina All-spice.
C. nànus, Loisel. (C. lævagàtus, Willd.)

Flowers, reddish-brown, solitary in the axils of the leaves, fragrant when crushed. *Petals* and *sepals*, similar in color, lance-shape, rather thick and fleshy, numerous in several rows, and all united below into a fleshy cup or tube. *Stamens*, usually about twelve. *Seed-cases*, few or many, enclosed in the calyx-tube. May, August.

Saxifrage (Saxifragaceæ)

Leaves, simple, opposite, entire, without stipules, oblong, thin. *Apex*, blunt or taper-pointed, smooth or nearly so on both sides.

Fruit, many times larger than that of the rose, which it somewhat resembles, enclosing the one-seeded seed-case *(achenia)*, dry when ripe. A covered cluster of achenes.

Found, in Franklin County, Pennsylvania, and southward along the Alleghany Mountains.

A shrub with aromatic bark, foliage, and flowers. The flowers when crushed have a "strawberry" odor.

C. flóridus, with larger flowers and oval leaves downy beneath, is often found in cultivation, but wild only in the South.

16. Family SAXIFRAGÀCEÆ. (Saxifrage Fam.)

Flowers, in clusters. *Petals*, separate, four to five [absent in Hydrángea (1)], inserted with the stamens on the calyx. *Sepals*, as many as the petals. *Seed-case*, adherent to the calyx. *Young Seeds*, small, many.

Leaves, simple, alternate or opposite, toothed or lobed.
Fruit, one- to two-celled, many-seeded. A capsule or a berry.

GUIDE TO THE GENERA.

Leaves opposite.	(1) Hydrángea.
" alternate, edge fine-toothed ; Fruit, a capsule.	(2) Itea
" " " lobed ; Fruit, a juicy berry.	(3) Ribes (Currant, etc.).

(1) Genus HYDRÁNGEA, L.

From two Greek words meaning "water" and "vase" because of the shape of the capsule.

Fig. 48.—Wild Hydrángea. *H. arboréscens, L.*

Flowers, in clusters, those in the margin usually without petals, stamens, or pistils, and with colored sepals; central flowers white, becoming rosy, fertile, with four or five egg-shaped petals, and twice as many stamens. *Styles*, two, diverging. *Seed-case*, two-beaked and adherent to the calyx-tube.

Leaves, opposite, toothed, without stipules, smooth or nearly so, egg-shape, or rarely heart-shaped. *Apex*, pointed.

Fruit, fifteen-ribbed, two-beaked, crowned with the two styles, two-celled in the lower part, opening by a hole between the beaks. A many-seeded capsule.

Found, from Pennsylvania westward and southward.

A very beautiful shrub, five or six feet high, often cultivated for its abundant flower clusters.

(2) Genus ÍTEA, Gronov.

Greek name of the "willow."

Fig. 49.—Ítea. *I. Virginica, L.*

Flowers, white, in somewhat spike-like, terminal clusters, small. *Petals*, five, separate, lance-shaped, much longer than the calyx. *Stamens*, five, shorter than the petals. May, June.

Leaves, simple, alternate, fine-toothed, with short stems, without stipules.

Fruit, oblong, two-grooved, two-celled, tipped with the two united styles, when ripe two-parted. *Seeds*, eight to twelve, oval and somewhat flattened. A capsule.

Found, in wet places, New Jersey and Pennsylvania, and southward.

A shrub about six feet high.

Fig. 48.—Wild Hydrángea. (H. arboréscens, L.)

Saxifrage (*Saxifragàceæ*)

(3) Genus RIBES, L. (Gooseberry, Currant.)

Flowers, small, white, greenish, or purple. *Petals*, five. *Stamens*, five. *Calyx*, often colored. *Seed-case*, united to the calyx, one-celled, many-seeded. *Styles*, two, distinct or united.

Leaves, simple, alternate, edges lobed, the lobes more or less toothed, folded fan-like in the bud. *Stem*, smooth in the currants, in the gooseberry with spines, and often with prickles.

Fruit, crowned with the remains of the calyx, many-seeded. A berry.

GUIDE TO THE SPECIES.

Flowers, greenish or purplish. Stems with thorns at the base of the leaf-stems, and usually with scattered prickles. (1 to 5) gooseberries.
Flowers, whitish. Stems without thorns or prickles. (6 and 7) currants.

Fig. 50.—(1) **Prickly Gooseberry.** *R. cynósbati, L.*

Flowers, greenish-white, drooping in clusters of one to three blossoms. *Lobes of the calyx*, much shorter than its tube. *Stamens*, and undivided *Style*, not longer than the calyx. May, June.

Leaves, three- to five-lobed. *Leaf-stem*, downy. *Stems*, mostly without scattered prickles, but with one to three spines near the axil of each leaf.

Fruit, large, usually armed with long prickles, brownish-purple; edible.

Found, from the mountains of North Carolina northward and westward; common.

A shrub about four feet high.

(2) **Common Wild Gooseberry.** *R. oxyacanthòides, L.*

Flowers, greenish or purplish, in drooping clusters of one to three blossoms. *Lobes of the calyx* much longer than the short tube. *Stamens*, scarcely as long as the broadly oblong calyx-lobes. *Style*, two-cleft. *Flower-stems*, short. May, June.

Leaves, roundish, heart-shaped, three- to five-lobed. *Spines,*

Fig. 49.—Ítea. (I. Virgínica, L.)
Fig. 50.—Prickly Gooseberry. (R. cynósbati, L.)

whitish, and often numerous. *Old bark*, often pealing off and leaving the stems unarmed.

Fruit, smooth, purple, sweet.

Found, from Newfoundland to New Jersey, and westward.

(3) Round-Leaved Gooseberry. *R. rotundifolium, Michx.*

This species differs from the common wild gooseberry chiefly in these items:

Stamens, somewhat longer than the spatulate-oblong calyx-lobes.

Leaves, roundish, and not usually heart-shaped at base.

Found, from western Massachusetts and New York southward.

(4) Missouri Gooseberry. *R. grácile, Michx.*

This species differs from the common wild gooseberry chiefly in these items:

Stamens, becoming much longer than the narrowly oblong calyx-lobes.

Leaves, roundish.

Spines, often long, stout, and red.

Found, from Michigan to Tennessee, and westward.

Fig. 51.—(5) Swamp Gooseberry. *R. lacústre, Poir.*

Flowers, in a drooping cluster of five to eight blossoms, greenish, small, flattened. *Stamens* and style not longer than the petals. *Style*, two-cleft. May.

Leaves, heart-shaped, three- to five-lobed. *Young stems*, covered thickly with reddish prickles and with slim thorns. *Old stems*, slightly armed with a few spines.

Fruit, dark-purple, small, bristly, unpleasant to the taste.

Found, in cold woods and swamps from New England northward and westward.

Saxifrage (Saxifragaceæ)

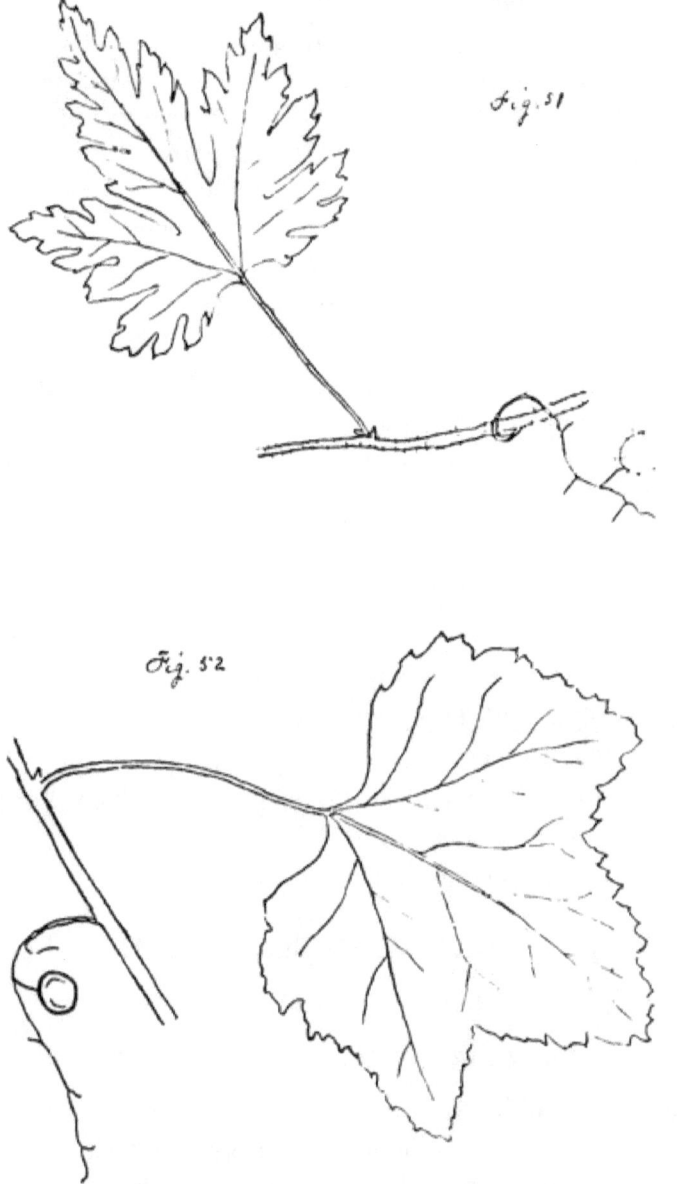

Fig. 51.—Swamp Gooseberry. (R. lacústre, Poir.)
Fig. 52.—Wild Red Currant. (R. rùbrum, L., var. subglandulòsum, Maxim.)

(6) **Wild Black Currant.** *R. flóridum, L'Her.*

Flowers, large, whitish, in drooping, downy clusters of many blossoms. *Calyx*, tubular, bell-shape, smooth. *Petals*, fringed toward the base. *Stamens*, short. *Flower-stems*, downy. *Bracts*, narrow, and longer than the flower-stems. May, June.

Leaves, three- to five-lobed, the surface marked on both sides with yellowish, resinous dots. *Stems*, without thorns or prickles, grayish.

Fruit, somewhat egg-shape, insipid, black, and smooth.

Found, in woods and hedges from New England to Virginia, and westward.

A handsome and common bush three to four feet high.

Fig. 52.—(7) **Wild Red Currant.** *R. rùbrum, L., var. subglandulósum, Maxim.*

This species differs from the Black Currant *(R. flóridum)* chiefly in these items:

Flower-clusters, less downy. *Calyx*, flat.

Leaves, often with less pointed lobes.

Fruit, round, red.

Found, in swamps and damp woods from New Jersey northward and westward.

A shrub with straggling and sometimes reclining stems.

17. Family HAMAMELÍDEÆ. (Witch-Hazel Fam.)

Genus HAMAMÈLIS, L.

Fig. 53.—**Witch Hazel.** *H. Virgínica, L.*

Flowers, stemless, bright-yellow, in clusters of three to four blossoms, blooming profusely about the time of the ripening of the leaf. *Petals*, four, separate, about

Witch-Hazel (Hamamelideæ)

Fig. 53.—Witch-Hazel. (H. Virginica, L.)
(a) Fruit. (b) Flower-cluster. (c) Single blossom.

three quarters of an inch long, very narrow (strap-like) inserted on the calyx. *Sepals*, four, downy. *Stamens*, eight, very short, four of them perfect, with anthers, the others imperfect and scale-like. *Styles*, two, short. *Pistils*, two, united below, so forming a *seed-case* which is two-beaked, two-celled, two- to several-seeded, and partly adherent to the calyx. The brown scale-like remains of the flower envelopes remain in the axils of the leaves of the next year. October, November.

Leaves, simple, alternate, edge strongly wavy, at times with some of the waves sharpened, three to five inches long, rounded, oval, or inversely egg-shape. *Base*, slightly heart-shaped and unequal. *Apex*, sometimes round and sometimes with a slight blunted point, sometimes roughened with small brown hairs along the back of the veins, shiny underneath, dark green above, veins straight.

Fruit, two-celled, with two large, hard seeds (a favorite food of the partridges), ripening in the summer from the previous autumn's flowers. A nut-like capsule. September.

Found, in damp woods, very widely distributed.

A shrub six to twelve feet high, with long straggling stems and branches, well worthy of cultivation because of its uniqueness throughout.

Riding one day in a slow stage across the hills of Central New York, a fellow-passenger—a lady—gave me this bit of information: "Once when my grandfather was seriously sick, there came to visit him an Oneida Indian, who prescribed for him to his great relief. Afterward he

Witch-Hazel (Hamamelidea)

learned from the Indian what the medicine was,—that it was an extract of Witch-Hazel, and received directions for its preparation. He prepared it and sold it very widely, calling it from his own name 'Pond's Extract.' Now the receipt and all rights are held by a New York and London Company called the 'Pond's Extract Co.'"

One reason for the popular name of the plant is faith in its power of indicating the presence of hidden springs. A man slowly paces the ground holding a switch of the hazel. Presently he thinks he feels the stick turning strongly in his grasp. He digs at the spot indicated, very likely finds water—if he digs far enough,—and so has his belief confirmed.

The slender branches are very tough—"awful tough, so 's you can tie up rails with 'em"—as a man once described them to me.

"Among the crimson and yellow hues of the falling leaves, there is no more remarkable object than the Witch-Hazel in the moment of parting with its foliage, putting forth a profusion of showy yellow blossoms, and giving to November the counterfeited appearance of spring."

It is by far the most unique and weird-like of all our shrubs. It deserves its name.

> You tangled bush
> With frost-killed leaves, and yellow flowers
> That outward push
> In spite of ice and autumn hours :
> You weird, wild thing o'-th'-woods
> Yclept witch-hazel, broods
> A ghoul, I fear,
> Within you here,

With witch-power fell,
   That's proof 'gainst book and **bell** ;—
Else how, 'mid early ice and snow
   And killing cold,
Can petal-lines of living gold
   Unfold them so ?
Unless, indeed, you hazel **wild**,
   Your heart like mine,
Has learned at last the lesson **mild**,
   The law divine,
   That ice nor snow
   Nor winds that blow
   Can freeze the flowers
      That glow
In happy hearts, and hazel bowers,—
That glow alike in darkest night
   And days of light ;
You hazel-bush, whose yellow flowers,
Are spring-time smiles in autumn hours.

18. Family ARALIACEÆ. (Ginseng Fam.)

Genus ARALIA, Tourn.

Fig. 54.—Angelica Tree. Hercules' Club. Devil's Walking-Stick. *A. spinòsa, L.*

Flowers, small and whitish, in large loose clusters above the leaves at the top of the tree. *Petals*, five, not united. *Stamens*, five, alternate with the petals. *Styles*, five. *Seed-case*, adherent to the calyx, five-celled, five-seeded. July, August.

Leaves, twice or thrice compound, odd-feathered, alternate, about three feet long and one and one half feet wide. *Leaflets*, very numerous, one and a half to three inches long, sharp-toothed, egg-shape. *Base*, rounded or slightly heart-shaped. *Apex*, pointed, very prickly, rough above and below. *Leaf-stem* and *leaflet-stems*,

Fig. 54.—Angelica Tree. (A. spinòsa, L.)
Part of the compound leaf.

beset with remote prickles. *Stems* and *branches*, set
with short, stout prickles.

Fruit, black or dark purple, five-celled, five-seeded,
crowned with the remains of the calyx and styles.
A berry-like drupe.

Found, on river banks and in damp woods, Pennsylvania,
and Ohio, and southward, and often in cultivation.

A shrub or small tree eight to twelve feet high, with
the great compound leaves mostly crowded toward the
ends of the branches, and fierce with its club-like prickly
stems. In the South it gains a height sometimes of
twenty to thirty feet, with straight, bare trunk, showing a
more palm-like style than any other of our trees.

19. Family CORNACEÆ. (Dogwood Fam.)

Genus CORNUS, Tourn. (Dogwood, Cornel.)

From a word meaning "horn," referring to the hardness of the wood.

Flowers, whitish, small, in flat or convex clusters. *Petals,*
four, not united, oblong, spreading. *Calyx,* minutely
four-toothed. *Stamens,* four. *Style,* one. *Seed-case,*
one, adherent to the calyx, two-celled, two-seeded.

Leaves, simple, opposite (except in *C. alternifòlia*), entire.
Veins, prominent, strongly and regularly curved.
Bark, bitter and tonic.

Fruit, small, rounded, crowned with the remains of the
flowers; berry-like, with a two-celled and two-seeded
stone. A berry-like drupe.

Fig. 55. –Round-Leaved Cornel. Round-Leaved Dogwood.
C. circinàta, L'Her.

Flowers, in flat loose clusters. June.

Leaves, round, oval, three to five inches long, larger than
in any other of the Dogwoods, thickly white woolly
beneath. *Branches,* greenish, dotted with warts.

Fruit, light blue, soft, hollow at the base. September.

Dogwood (Cornaceæ)

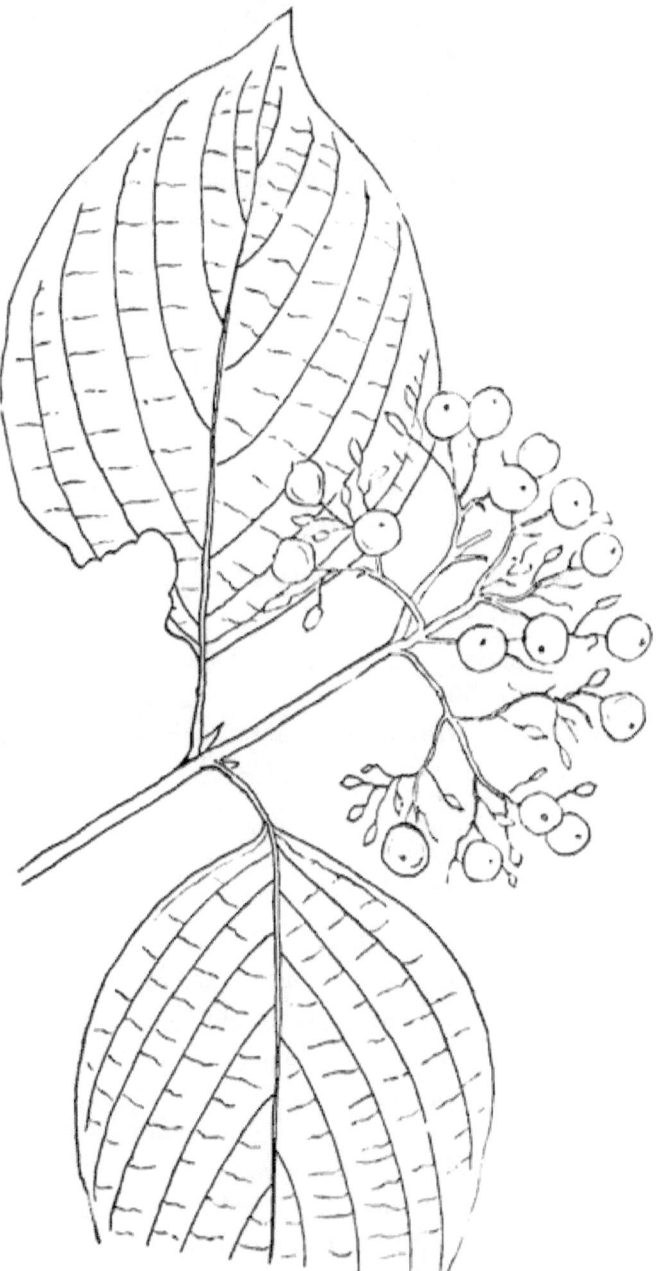

Fig. 55.—Round-Leaved Cornel. (C. circinàta, L'Her.)

Dogwood (Cornaceæ)

Found, from Maryland westward and northward, on shady banks, and in thickets.

A shrub four to ten feet high, with straight and slender branches.

Silky Cornel or Dogwood. Kinnikinnik. *C. sericea, L.*

Flowers, in flat and close clusters. June.

Leaves, two to four inches long and half as broad, narrow egg-shape to lance-shape. *Base*, rounded and sometimes tapering, silky downy beneath. *Branches*, purplish. *Young shoots*, dark red. *Branchlets* and *stalks*, silky downy.

Fruit, blue.

Found, in wet ground, United States and Canada.

A shrub three to ten feet high.

Long-Leaved Cornel or Dogwood. *C. asperifolia, Michx.*

Flowers, in flat clusters.

Leaves, egg-shape and oblong. *Apex*, pointed. *Base*, rounded or pointed, rough above, soft downy beneath. *Leaf-stem*, rough and rather short. *Branches*, brownish. *Branchlets*, rough.

Fruit, white, rounded, often with red stems.

Found, from the northern shore of Lake Erie to Minnesota, and southward.

A tall shrub.

Red-Osier Dogwood or Cornel. *C. stolonifera, Michx.*

Flowers, in small, flat, and smooth clusters of rather few and loosely arranged blossoms.

Leaves, broad egg-shape. *Base*, rounded. *Apex*, short-pointed, minutely downy above, whitish downy beneath. *Branches* and *branchlets*, smooth; the *shoots* (and usually the branches) reddish-purple—toward the end of winter almost blood-red.

Fruit, white or bluish-white.

Found, in wet places; common, especially northward.

A shrub three to six feet high, with slender, spreading branches. It multiplies freely by sending up long, wand-like shoots—"suckers"—soon forming broad clumps.

Panicled Cornel or Dogwood. *C. candidissima*, Marsh. *C. paniculata*, L'Her.

Flowers, in many small, loose, convex, or cone-shaped clusters. May, June.

Leaves, one to three inches long, egg-shape to long oval. *Apex*, taper-pointed. *Base*, acute or rounded, whitish beneath, not downy. *Branches*, grayish, smooth. *Shoots*, chestnut-color.

Fruit, white, rounded, the size of peas, with the stalk, when ripe, of a pale scarlet. August, September.

Found, in thickets, along river banks, etc.; common.

A shrub four to ten feet high, much branching, showy, with its abundant flower and fruit clusters.

Alternate-Leaved Cornel or Dogwood. *C. alternifolia*, L. f.

Flowers, in wide open clusters. May, June.

Leaves, alternate, mostly clustered at the ends of the branches, egg-shape to reverse egg-shape. *Apex*, pointed. *Base*, pointed, minutely downy beneath. *Branches*, greenish, oftenest marked with white, warty streaks.

Fruit, rounded, deep blue or black on reddish fruit-stalks, much liked by the birds. August.

Found, from Georgia and Alabama, northward and westward.

A shrub or small tree ten to twenty feet high, beautiful in cultivation. The bark forms one of the "Quaker medicines," being considered diaphoretic and astringent.

CLASS FIRST—Continued

(*Angiospermæ*)

Division II
PETALS MOSTLY UNITED

(*Gamopetalous*)

20. Family CAPRIFOLIACEÆ. (Honeysuckle Fam.)

Flowers, variously clustered. *Corolla* of united petals, tubular or wheel-shaped, inserted on the calyx. *Stamens*, as many as the lobes of the corolla, and inserted on it. *Seed-case*, two- to five-celled, adherent to the calyx.
Leaves, simple or compound, opposite.
Fruit, a berry, drupe, or capsule.

Guide to the Genera.

(a) Leaves compound.   (1) Sambúcus (Elders).
(a) Leaves simple, toothed or lobed (except in Withe-rod) corolla regular, fruit a one-seeded drupe.   (2) Vibúrnum (Arrow-woods, etc.).
(a) Leaves simple, entire.
  (b) Corolla regular; fruit a two-seeded berry.   (3) Symphoricárpos (Snowberry, etc.).
  (c) Corolla irregular; fruit a two- to three-seeded berry.   (4) Lonicéra (Fly-Honeysuckles.)
(a) Leaves simple, toothed; corolla only slightly irregular; fruit a many-seeded capsule.   (5) Diervilla (Bush-Honeysuckle).

(1) Genus SAMBÚCUS, Tourn. (Elder.)

Fig. 56.—Common Elder. *S. Canadénsis, L.*

Flowers, white, small, with a heavy odor, in clusters that are flat, five to seven times parted, and five to eight inches in diameter. *Corolla*, five-cleft, with the lobes blunt. *Calyx*, small. *Stamens*, five. May, July.

Leaves, compound, opposite. *Leaflets*, five to eleven (oftenest seven), two to four inches long, egg-shape to oblong and reverse egg-shape, mostly smooth, the lower ones often two- or three-parted, with a rank

Fig. 56.—Common Elder. (S. Canadénsis, L.) (a) Flower enlarged.

odor when crushed. *Leaf-stems,* smooth. **Bark**, warty, that of the new shoots bright green, that of the older branches purplish-brown, or in winter light grayish. *Branches,* swollen at the joints. *Pith,* abundant and white.

Fruit, small, black-purple when ripe, round, pulpy, abundant, three-seeded, with dark, crimson juice. August, September.

Found, in waste places, often forming thickets; very common north, south, east, and west.

A shrub six to ten feet high, with weak, pithy, large-jointed branches. "In domestic medicine this plant forms almost a pharmacy in itself," flowers, leaves, leaf-buds, inner-bark, berries—all are used. Elder-blow tea (an infusion of the flowers), when cold, is alterative and laxative; when hot, an excitant. The inner bark is used in preparing ointments; the juice of the berries makes a cooling laxative drink, and is made also into a medicinal "elder-berry wine." The berries are used in cookery. The unopened flower-buds are pickled and used as a good substitute for "capers." An infusion of the juice forms a delicate test for the presence of acids and alkalies. The pith of the stems furnishes the best pith balls for electrical experiments.

Red-berried Elder. *S. pubens, Michx. S. racemosa. L.*

This species differs from the preceding chiefly in the following items:

Flowers, in egg-shaped or pyramidal clusters. May.

Leaflets, five to seven (oftenest five), long oval to lance-

Honeysuckle (Caprifoliàceæ)

shape, more or less downy beneath, very downy when young.

Leaf-stem, downy beneath when young, often purple above. *Pith*, brown.

Fruit, bright red (or rarely white) with a yellowish, unpleasant-tasting pulp. June.

Found, from Georgia northward and westward.

A shrub two to eighteen feet high.

(2) Genus VIBÚRNUM, L. (Arrow-wood, etc.)

Flowers, white, in flat, compound clusters. *Corolla*, spreading, and deeply five-lobed. *Calyx*, five-toothed, the lobes blunt. *Stamens*, five. *Stigmas*, one to three. *Seed-cases*, one- to three-celled.

Leaves, simple, opposite, toothed (excepting in species No. 8, Withe-rod), lobed in No. 2, Cranberry Tree; No. 3, Few-Flowered Viburnum; and No. 4, Dockmackie.

Fruit, soft, pulpy, one-celled, one-seeded. A one-seeded drupe.

GUIDE TO THE SPECIES.

(*a*) Flower-clusters with the outer blossoms imperfect (destitute of stamens and pistils).
   (*b*) Leaves not lobed   (1) Hobble-Bush.
   (*b*) leaves three-lobed   (2) Cranberry Tree.
(*a*) Flower-clusters with the blossoms perfect and alike.
   (*b*) Leaves three-lobed   { (3) Few-Flowered Viburnum;
                                      { (4) Dockmackie.
   (*b*) Leaves not lobed.
       (*c*) Edge coarsely toothed, clusters { (5) Arrow-wood;
            stalked   { (6) Soft Viburnum;
                                       { (7) Downy Viburnum.
       (*c*) Edge entire or nearly so   { (8) Withe-rod (*V. nudum*);
                                       { (9) Withe-rod (*V. cassinoides*).
       (*c*) Edge fine-toothed, clusters sessile (10) Black Haw.

Honeysuckle (Caprifoliaceæ)

Fig. 57.—(1) Hobble-Bush.   American Wayfaring Tree.
V. lantanoides, Michx.

Flowers, in a sessile cluster, the outer ones showy and imperfect, lacking pistils and stamens, and with the flat corollas much enlarged (nearly one inch across); greenish, changing to white; with five rounded lobes; the inner flowers much smaller and perfect.   May.

Leaves, four to eight inches across.   *Veins and veinlets*, beneath, and the *leaf-stems* very brown-scurfy.

Fruit, egg-shape, bright red, becoming almost black, not acid.   *Stone*, grooved.   September.

Found, in cool, damp woods, from Pennsylvania northward.

A very straggling shrub about five feet high, its long, almost rope-like branches often reclining and taking root, so forming troublesome "hobbles" for any careless wayfarer among them.

Fig. 58.—(2) Bush Cranberry.   Cranberry Tree.   High Cranberry.   *V. ópulus, L.*

Flower-clusters, three to four inches across, resembling the last, but not sessile.   June, July.

Leaves, three and one half to five inches wide, strongly three-veined from the base; three-lobed, the lobes more or less toothed along the sides, entire in the hollows.   *Base*, broad, wedge-shaped, rounded, or squared.   *Leaf-stem*, with small, wart-like glands near the upper end.   *Stipules*, almost thread-like.

Fig. 57.—Hobble-Bush. (V. lantanoides, Michx.)

Honeysuckle (Caprifoliaceæ)

Fruit, about the size of a cranberry, round or egg-shape, light red, acid, ripening late and remaining after the leaves have fallen. *Stone*, very flat, not grooved. September.

Found, in borders of fields and along streams from Pennsylvania northward and westward.

A handsome shrub three to ten feet high, showy in flower and in fruit, well worthy of cultivation. The fruit, in appearance and in taste is somewhat like the cranberry, as a poor substitute for which it is often used.

The common garden "snowball" or "Guelder rose" is a cultivated form of this species, with all the blossoms in the round clusters changed to the larger imperfect form,—clusters that are described by Cowper as

> "Silver globes, light as the foamy surf
> That the wind severs from the broken wave."

(3) **Few-Flowered Vibúrnum.**   *V. pauciflorum, Pylaie.*

Flowers, in small clusters of few blossoms on short side branches.

Leaves, somewhat three-lobed toward the end, rounded, mostly with five veins from the base.

Fruit, much as in the preceding species.

Found, occasionally in the mountains of New England, and northward and westward.

A small, straggling bush, nearly smooth throughout.

Honeysuckle (Caprifoliaceæ) 137

Fig. 58.—Bush Cranberry. (V. ópulus, L.)

Fig. 59.—(4) Dockmackie.   Maple-Leaved Arrow-wood.
V. acerifolium, L.

Flowers, all perfect, in small, flat, terminal, long-stemmed clusters. *Stamens*, extending beyond the corolla. May, June.

Leaves, two to four inches long, closely resembling in shape the leaf of the red maple; strongly three-veined from the base, soft-downy beneath. *Base*, rounded or heart-shaped. *Bark*, yellowish-green.

Fruit, crimson, changing to dark-purple or black, disagreeable to the taste. *Stone*, thin, of the shape of a double convex-lens, scarcely grooved.

Found, in cool woods from North Carolina northward and westward.

A shrub three to six feet high, the branches often straight and slender, "arrow-like," and ending with a pair of leaves and the flower-cluster.

Fig. 60.—(5) Arrow-wood.   *V. dentatum, L.*

Flowers, perfect, clusters not sessile.   June.

Leaves, egg-shape to rounded, mostly smooth, coarsely toothed. *Veins*, beneath prominent, straight, and usually with downy tufts in their axils. *Base*, sometimes slightly heart-shaped. *Leaf-stems*, rather slender. *Young shoots*, mostly smooth. *Bark*, ash-colored; on old stems, nearly black.

Fruit, about one quarter inch long, slightly lengthened, dark blue. *Stone*, very deeply grooved.

Found, in damp woods and thickets from Northern Georgia northward and westward; not uncommon.

A shrub five to fifteen feet high, often with straight, arrow-like shoots.

Honeysuckle (Caprifoliaceæ)

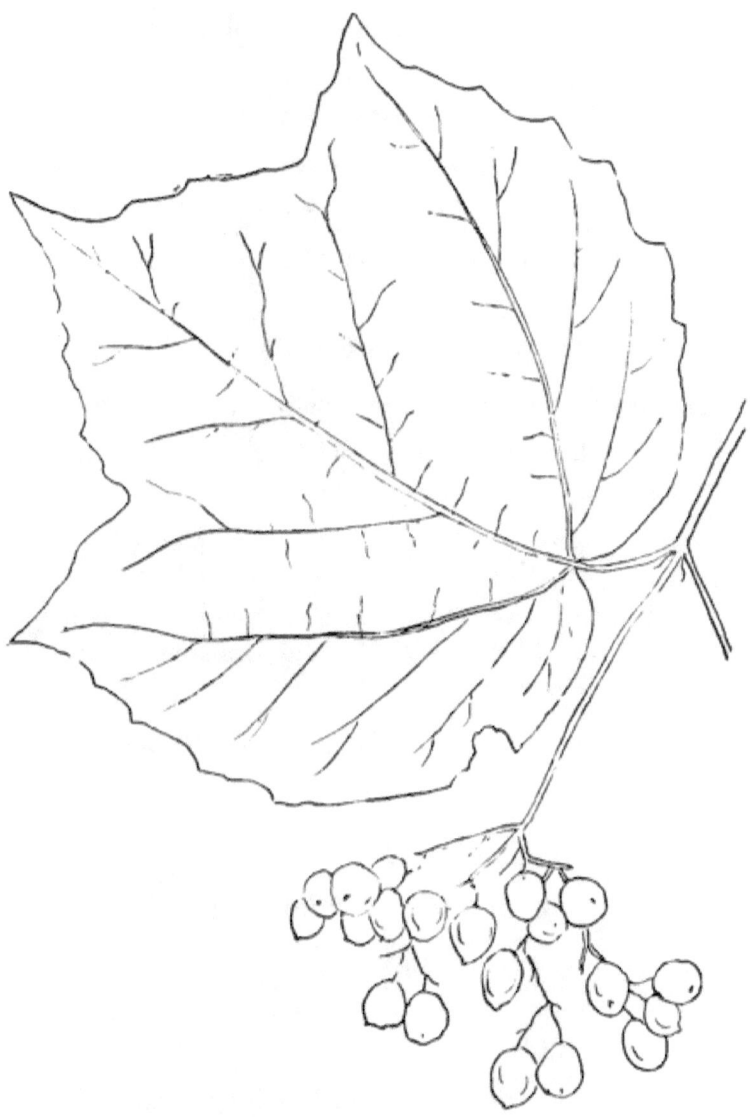

Fig. 59.—Maple-Leaved Arrow-wood. (V. acerifòlium, L.)

(6) **Soft Viburnum.** *V. molle, Michx.*

This species differs from the preceding chiefly in the following items:

Flowers, rather larger. *Clusters*, downy.

Leaves, egg-shape to reverse egg-shape, downy beneath. *Young shoots* and branchlets, downy.

Fruit, larger and more pointed. *Stones*, rather less deeply grooved.

Found, from Martha's Vineyard southward.

Fig. 61.—(7) **Downy Arrow-wood.** *V. pubéscens, Pursh.*

Flowers, rather larger than in *V. dentàtum*. *Clusters*, small and few-flowered. June.

Leaves, egg-shape. *Apex*, pointed or long-pointed. *Veins*, less marked than in *V. dentàtum*. *Leaf-stems*, very short, with two short, hairy, stipule-like appendages at base. Leaves beneath and leaf-stem downy, at least when young.

Fruit, nearly black. *Stone*, flat and slightly grooved on each side.

Found, in dry woods and thickets from Georgia northward.

A straggling shrub about six feet high.

Fig. 62.—(8) **Withe-rod.** *V. nùdum, L.*

Flowers, in large clusters with a stem one to two inches long. April, June.

Leaves, variable, two to four inches long, oval to lance-shape, edge entire or obscurely toothed, often slightly rolled; smooth, not shining, no stipule-like append-

Honeysuckle (Caprifoliàceæ) 141

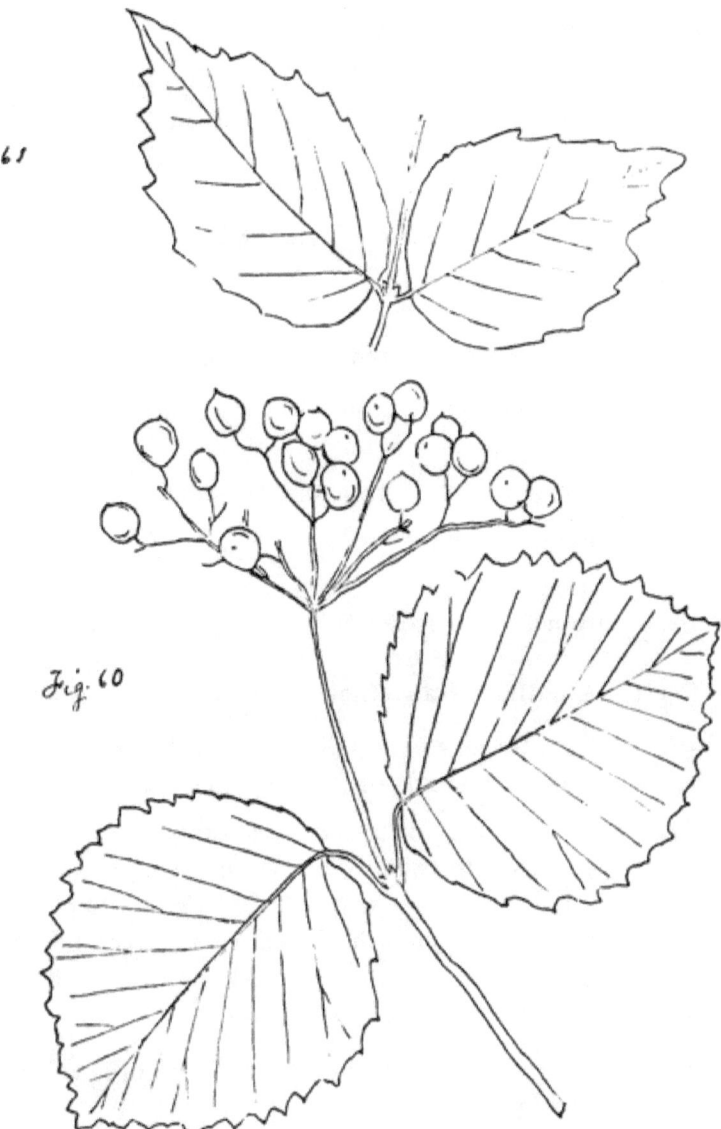

Fig. 60.—Arrow-wood. (V. dentàtum, L.)
Fig. 61.—Downy Arrow-wood. (V. pubéscens, Pursh.)

ages. *Shoots, branchlets,* etc., often slightly scurfy-dotted.

Fruit, about one quarter inch long, slightly lengthened, blackish, sweet. *Stone,* broadly oval or round, very flat and even.

Found, from New Jersey southward.

A very variable shrub (or sometimes a small tree) ten to twenty feet high.

(9) **Withe-rod.** *V. cassinoïdes, L.*

This species differs from the preceding *(V. nùdum)* chiefly in the following items:

Flower-cluster, usually with a shorter stem.

Leaves, one to three inches long.

Shoots, scurfy-dotted.

Found, from New Jersey northward and westward.

Fig. 63.—(10) **Black Haw. Sloe. Stag-Bush.** *V. prunifòlium, L.*

Flowers, in rather large and flat three- to five-rayed sessile clusters at the ends of the branches. May.

Leaves, one to three inches long, smooth, shining above, broadly-oval to broadly-reverse egg-shape, finely and sharply toothed. *Apex,* rounded or pointed. *Leaf-stem,* short and smooth, the edges slightly and evenly winged; variable.

Fruit, oval, blackish, sweet and eatable.

Found, in Connecticut and Southern New York, westward to Michigan, and southward.

A bush (or a small tree) ten to twenty feet high. The bark is sometimes used as a tonic.

Fig. 62.—Withe-rod. (V. nùdum, L.)
Fig. 63.—Black Haw. (V. prunifòlium, L.)

Honeysuckle (Caprifoliàceæ)

(3) Genus SYMPHORICÁRPOS, Dill. (Snowberry, etc.)

<small>From Greek words meaning "to bear together" and "fruit," because of the clustered berries.</small>

Flowers, white with a rosy or purplish tinge in clusters or spikes, or sometimes solitary. *Corolla*, bell-shaped, four- to five-lobed. *Calyx*, with short teeth. *Stamens*, four or five, inserted on the throat of the corolla. *Stigma*, rounded. *Seed-case*, four-celled, but with only two of the cells containing perfect young seeds.

Leaves, simple, broad-oval to oblong, opposite, edge entire.

Fruit, with four cells and two seeds. A berry.

Fig. 64.—Snowberry. *S. racemòsus, Michx.*

Flowers, in a loose and often somewhat leafy terminal spike. *Corolla*, thickly-bearded within. *Stamens* and style not longer than the corolla tube ("included"). *Style*, smooth. June, August.

Leaves, smooth or nearly so, often with wavy margins.

Fruit, snow-white, the size of a large pea.

Found, native in New England and Pennsylvania, and northward and westward, and in cultivation.

A pretty bush two to three feet high, very common in cultivation, especially in old gardens, attractive, not on account of its flowers, but its white fruit.

Var. pauciflorus, Robbins, has the flower spike reduced to only one or two blossoms.

Wolf-berry. *S. occidentàlis, Hook.*

Flowers, crowded in nodding terminal or axillary spikes. *Corolla*, bearded within. *Stamens* and *Style*, longer than the corolla-tube ("exserted"). July.

Honeysuckle (Caprifoliaceæ)

Fig. 64.—Snowberry. (S. racemòsus, Michx.)
Fig. 65.—Indian Currant. (S. orbiculàris, Moench.)

Leaves, one to three inches long.
Fruit, white.
Found, from Illinois northward and westward.
  A shrub two to four feet high.

Fig. 65.—**Indian Currant. Coral-berry.** *S. orbiculàris*, *Moench*
(*S. vulgàris*, *Michx.*)

Flowers, crowded in short clusters in the axils of most of the leaves. *Corolla*, only slightly bearded within. *Stamens* and style shorter than the corolla-tube ("included"). *Style*, bearded. July.
Leaves, round-oval, one to two inches long, nearly stemless.
Fruit, small, dark red.
Found, from Pennsylvania northward and southward.
  A shrub two to three feet high.

(4) Genus LONICÈRA, L. (Fly-Honeysuckle.)

Flowers, in pairs in the axils of the leaves, each pair with a single stalk. *Corolla*, tubular or funnel-like, often hairy at the base within, five-lobed, more or less irregular. *Stamens*, five, longer than the corolla-tube ("exserted"). *Seed-case*, two- to three-celled.
Leaves, simple, opposite, entire.
Fruit, a several-seeded berry.

Fig. 66.—**Fly-Honeysuckle.** *L. ciliàta* *Muhl.*

Flowers, greenish-yellow, three quarters inch long. *Corolla*, funnel-form, slightly, blunt, spurred at the base. *Petals*, nearly equal. *Bracts*, two, minute at the base of the seed-case. *Stem* of the pair of flowers, slender, shorter than the leaves. May, June.

Honeysuckle (Caprifoliàceæ)

Fig. 66.—Fly-Honeysuckle. (L. ciliàta, Muhl.) (a) Fruit.

Honeysuckle (Caprifoliaceæ)

Leaves, from long egg-shape to oval. *Base,* variable, rounded, or slightly pointed, or often heart-shaped; thin, delicately fringed on the margin. *Leaf-stem,* slightly hairy.

Fruit, red, oblong, or egg-shape, in pairs, three- to five-seeded, distinct or sometimes slightly united.

Found, in woods from Pennsylvania northward and westward.

A shrub three to six feet high, with straggling branches set at a very wide angle.

Mountain-Fly Honeysuckle. *L. cerulea, L.*

Flowers, yellowish. *Bracts,* two, at the base of the seed-case, awl-shaped, longer than the seed-case. *Stem* of the pair of flowers, very short—shorter than the flowers. May, June.

Leaves, small, egg-shape or oval to reverse egg-shape; hairy, especially when young.

Fruit, dark blue, the two berries united into one.

Found, in high woods from Rhode Island northward and westward.

A shrub one to three feet high.

Swamp Fly-Honeysuckle. *L. oblongifolia, Muhl.*

Flowers, yellowish-white outside, purplish within, one half inch long, deeply two-lipped. *Corolla,* hairy. *Bracts,* two, minute or soon falling. *Stem* of the pair of flowers, slender, as long as the leaves. June.

Leaves, one to three inches in length, oblong, nearly stemless.

Honeysuckle (Caprifoliàceæ)

Fruit, rounded, purple, the two berries more or less parted at the summit, or sometimes nearly distinct.

Found, in swampy land, from New York northward and westward.

A shrub three to four feet high.

Bracted Fly-Honeysuckle. *L. involucràta, Banks.*

Flowers, yellowish. *Corolla*, one half to three quarters of an inch long, slightly sticky. *Stem* of the pair of flowers shorter than the leaves.

Leaves, two to five inches long, egg-shape or oblong, mostly pointed. *Branches*, four-angled.

Fruit, rounded, dark-purple, the two berries distinct.

Found, in deep woods from the shores of Lake Superior north and west.

Tartarian Honeysuckle. [*L. Tartárica, L.*]

Flowers, pale-purple to white, small, fragrant. April, June.

Leaves, one to two inches long, three quarters to one and one half inches wide, thick, egg-shape. *Base*, heart-shaped. *Apex*, blunt, smooth, shining, dark-green above. *Leaf-stem*, short.

Found, common in cultivation, naturalized in the vicinity of New York.

Honeysuckle (*Caprifoliàceæ*)

A shrub four to ten feet high, with erect, much-branching stems; elegant, and every way worthy of cultivation. Introduced from Russia.

(5) Genus DIERVÍLLA, Tourn.

Fig. 67.—**Bush Honeysuckle.** *D. trifida (L.) Moench.*

Flowers, greenish-yellow, in clusters that are either terminal or in the axils of the upper leaves—usually three blossoms to each flower-stem. *Corolla*, funnel-form, five-lobed, nearly regular, twice as long as the calyx. *Calyx-lobes*, slender, awl-shaped, persistent. *Stamens*, five; stamens and style much longer than the tube of the corolla. *Seed-case*, slender, about one third inch long.

Leaves, simple, opposite, two to four inches in length, long egg-shape, toothed, taper-pointed. *Stems*, marked with two slight ridges, very noticeable in the young shoots.

Fruit, tapering above into a slender beak, which is often curved, and is crowned with the long and somewhat spreading persistent sepals. *Cells*, two (apparently four because of the intruding false partitions). *Seeds*, many. A capsule.

Found, from the mountains of North Carolina northward and westward.

An upright shrub about two feet high, very modest as compared with its showy related species, the cultivated Japanese "Weigela."

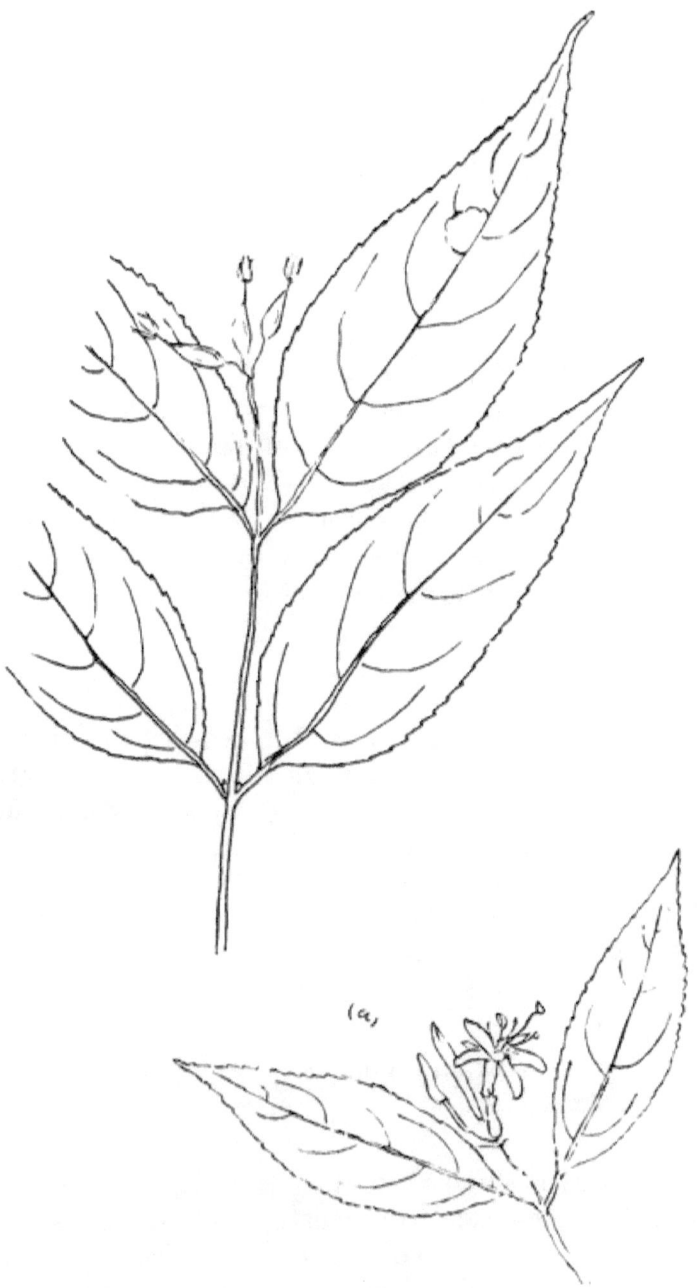

Fig. 67.—Bush Honeysuckle. D. trifida (L.), Moench. (a) Flower-cluster.

Madder (*Rubiaceæ*)

21. Family RUBIACEÆ. (Madder Fam.)

Genus CEPHALÁNTHUS, L.

From two Greek words meaning "head" and "a flower," referring to the arrangement of the round flower-clusters.

Fig. 68.—Button-Bush. *C. occidentális, L.*

Flowers, white, in dense spherical heads—each head nearly an inch in diameter, on a long stalk. *Corolla*, with united petals, tubular, four-toothed. *Calyx-tube*, inversely pyramid-shaped. *Stamens*, four, inserted on the tube of the corolla. *Style*, much exserted, long, and thread-like—nearly twice as long as the corolla. *Seed-case*, adherent to the calyx. July, August.

Leaves, variable, three to five inches long, simple, opposite (often whorled in threes), egg-shape to oblong, and reverse egg-shape, edge entire, strongly veined. *Base*, pointed or rounded. *Stipules*, short, connecting the bases of the opposite leaf-stems.

Fruit, small, inversely pyramid-shaped, dry and hard. *Cells*, two to four, each with one seed, splitting from the base upwards. September.

Found, in swamps and along streams of United States and Canada.

A vigorous shrub about four feet high. It is sometimes found on elevated ground, where it serves, it is claimed, as a good sign of the presence of hidden springs. The inner bark is sometimes used as a cough medicine.

Fig. 68.—Button-Bush. (C. occidentàlis, L.)
Fig. 69.—Groundsel Tree. (B. halimifòlia, L.)

22. Family COMPÓSITÆ. (Composite Fam.)
Genus BÁCCHARIS, L.

From "the name of the god Bacchus, possibly because of a faint wine-like odor about the plant."

Fig. 69.—Groundsel Tree. *B. halimifòlia, L.*

Flowers, whitish or yellow, tubular, in a close head of about twenty blossoms, the staminate and the pistillate forms on different bushes. *Corolla*, of the pistillate flower thread-like; of the staminate, larger and five-lobed; the hairy pappus of the pistillate flowers long and very abundant. September.

Leaves, simple, alternate, edge mostly remotely large-toothed (in the upper leaves often entire), reverse egg-shape to lanceolate. *Branches*, angled.

Fruit, one-seeded, a ribbed akene.

Found, near the sea, from Massachusetts to Georgia.

A compact shrub six to twelve feet high, worthy of cultivation because of its late blooming and its abundant "white-haired" blossoms.

Genus ÌVA, L.

Marsh Elder. Highwater Shrub. *I. frutéscens, L.*

Flowers, greenish-white, tubular or funnel-form, in small, drooping heads, each head with fine marginal, pistillate flowers, the remaining flowers staminate, pappus lacking. July to September.

Leaves, simple, fleshy, the lower ones opposite, lance-shaped, and coarsely toothed, the upper ones narrower and with entire edges, or reduced to line-like bracts.

Fruit, one-seeded (five seeds to each head). An akene.

Found, on the borders of salt marshes from Massachusetts to Florida; common.

A coarse, leafy shrub, three to eight feet high.

Heath (Ericàceæ)

23. Family ERICÀCEÆ. (Heath Fam.)

Flowers, regular, or nearly so, except in *R. Rhodòra* (8). *Petals*, four to five, united, except in *R. Rhodòra* (8), *Ledum* (9), and *Clethra* (10). *Stamens*, usually as many to twice as many as the petals, and inserted with them. *Pollen*, of four united grains. *Style*, one. *Seed-case*, three- to ten-celled.

Leaves, simple, without stipules.

Fruit, a berry or a capsule.

There are not many families that contain as many beautiful plants as are found among the *Ericàceæ*. Of the true heaths, however, we have no native species. The nearest to them are our huckleberries and cranberries. These take the place throughout the northern part of America of the heaths of the corresponding climate of Europe, and they do so with as much of beauty and with far more of usefulness.

A Guide to the Genera.

(*A*) Calyx adherent to seed-case; Fruit a berry, crowned with the calyx-teeth.
  (*b*) Fruit ten-seeded   (1) Gaylussàcia (Huckleberry).
  (*b*) " many-seeded   (2) Vaccinium (Blueberry, etc.).
(*A*) Calyx not adherent to seed-case; Fruit a many-seeded capsule.
  (*b*) Petals always regular, and all united.
    (*c*) Corolla cylindrical, or contracted at its mouth; Fruit, more or less globular to egg-shape.
        (3) Andrómeda.
        (4) Leucóthoë.
        (5) Cassándra.
        (7) Menziéna.
    (*c*) Corolla saucer-shape, with ten hollows for holding the anthers. Leaves, thick and evergreen.
        (6) Kálmia (Laurels, etc.).
  (*b*) Petals sometimes irregular, and in *R. Rhodòra* partly separate. Corolla, spreading, funnel-shape, or bell-shape.
        (8) Rhododéndron (Azaleas, etc.).
  (*b*) Petals regular and separate.
    (*c*) Leaves very woolly beneath, edge entire.
        (9) Ledum (Labrador Tea).
    (*c*) Leaves, smooth, edge-toothed.   (10) Clethra (Sweet Pepper-bush.)

Heath (Ericàceæ)

(1) Genus GAYUSSACIA, H. B. K. (Huckleberry.)

Flowers, white or tinged with red, in loose lateral clusters. *Corolla*, egg-shape, tubular, or bell-shape; five-lobed. *Calyx*, yellowish-green, with resinous dots. *Stamens*, ten. *Anther-cells*, tapering upward, and opening by a chink at the end, with no small hooks at the back. *Seed-case*, ten-celled and ten-seeded, adherent to the calyx.

Leaves, alternate, entire (excepting in Box Huckleberry, and sometimes in Dwarf Huckleberry), and more or less resinous dotted (excepting in Box Huckleberry).

Fruit, black or dark blue, round, ten-celled, ten-seeded, crowned with the teeth of the calyx. A berry.

Fig. 70.—**Common Black Huckleberry.** *G. resinòsa (Ait.)*, *T. and G.*

Flowers, drooping, in short, one-sided clusters. *Corolla*, contracted at the mouth, longer than the stamens, shorter than the style. *Bracts* of the flower-clusters, small, reddish, and soon falling away. *Flower-stems*, each about the length of the blossom. May, June.

Leaves, one to two and one half inches long, entire, egg-shape and oval to reverse egg-shape, pointed or somewhat blunt, thickly sprinkled—more thickly than are any other of the huckleberries—with bright resinous globules.

Fruit, black (very rarely white), sweet. August.

Found, from Northern Georgia and Tennessee northward. Common in woods and open fields.

A stiff, much-branched shrub, one to three feet high, yielding the "huckleberry" of the markets.

Fig. 70.—Common Black Huckleberry. G. resinòsa (Ait.), Torr. and Gray.
Fig. 71.—Dangleberry. G. frondòsa (L.), Torr. and Gray.

Heath (Ericàceæ)

The "huckleberry pasture" is an important part of many a New England farm, and the name is a well remembered one in the memory of many a far wanderer from his early home. Those who know the stout and thickly set bushes, and who know also the ideal Christian character of many of the New England settlers, can appreciate the comment of an old lady (quoted by Ralph Waldo Emerson), who, remembering her godly ancestors, said of them "that they had to hold on hard by the huckleberry bushes to hinder themselves from being translated."

A peculiar old and shorter name for huckleberries is "hurts."

"Cape Cod is only a headland of high hills overgrowne with shrubby pines, *hurts*, and such trash, but an excellent harbour of all weathers."—Capt. JOHN SMITH, Work II.

Dwarf Huckleberry. *G. dumòsa (Andr.), T. and G.*

Flowers, each from the axil of a persistent bract, in somewhat lengthened clusters. *Bracts*, leaf-like, oval, as long as the flower-stem, and persistent. *Corolla*, bell-shape, with five prominent keel-like angles, longer than the included stamen and style. *Seedcase*, set with hairs or glands. June.

Leaves, about one and one third inches long, entire or slightly fine-toothed, reverse egg-shape, blunt, bristle-tipped. Leaves, branchlets, and flower-stems sprinkled with small hairs and glands.

Fruit, black, one third to one half inch in diameter, rather insipid. August.

Heath (Ericàceæ)

Found, in swamps and thickets from Canada to Florida, mostly along the coast.

A small shrub, usually about one foot high, from a creeping base.

Fig. 71.—Dangleberry. Blue Dangle. *G. frondòsa (L.), T. and G.*

Flowers, in slender, loose clusters. *Bracts*, oblong or line-like, soon falling, shorter than the slender and drooping flower-stems. *Corolla*, round, bell-shape, longer than the included stamens. May, June.

Leaves, entire, mostly reverse egg-shape, often blunt.

Fruit, large, blue, sweet, covered with a whitish bloom when ripe. July, August.

Found, from Newfoundland to Florida, oftenest in sandy swamps.

A loosely branching shrub, three to six feet high.

Box Huckleberry. *G. brachýcera, Gray.*

Flowers, in short, close, axillary, and terminal clusters. *Flower-stems*, very short. May.

Leaves, one inch long, oval, thick, smooth, many-toothed, evergreen, resembling the leaf of the box.

Fruit, light blue.

Found, in Perry County, Pennsylvania, and southward.

A pretty evergreen about one foot high.

(2) Genus VACCÍNIUM, L. (Blueberry, etc.)

This genus differs from *Gaylussàcia* chiefly in the following items :

Flowers, with *corolla* five-toothed, excepting in Bog Bilberry, where it is four-toothed. *Anthers*, sometimes with two small, bristle-like hooks (awns) on the back. *Seed-case*, four-celled (or sometimes eight- to ten-celled by false divisions), many-seeded.

Leaves, branchlets, etc., less strongly or not at all marked with resinous globules.

Fruit, four- to five-celled (or sometimes eight- to ten-celled by false divisions), and many-seeded instead of only ten-seeded.

Fig. 72.—Squaw Huckleberry. Deerberry. *V. stamineum*, L.

Flowers, nodding, greenish-white or purplish. *Flower-stems*, slender, solitary in the axils of the leaves. *Stamens*, hairy, shorter than the style, much exserted from the corolla. *Anthers*, tapering into two horns, with a hook (awn) back of each.

Leaves, one and one half to two and one half inches long, rounded or pointed, or sometimes heart-shaped at base; smallest on the flowering branches; egg-shape and oval to reverse egg-shape. *Leaf-stem*, very short and downy.

Fruit, somewhat ten-celled, nearly as large as a small cherry, greenish or yellowish, sometimes purple-tinged, round or pear-shaped, scarcely edible. September.

Found, from Canada to Florida.

A shrub two to three feet high with abundant spreading branches and drooping solitary fruit.

Heath (Ericàceæ)

Fig. 72.—Squaw Huckleberry. (V. stamineum, L.)
Fig. 73.—Common Low Blueberry. (V. Pennsylvánicum, Lam.)

Heath (Ericàceæ)

Fig. 73.— Common Low Blueberry. Dwarf Blueberry.
V. Pennsylvánicum, Lam.

Flowers, usually reddish-white, one quarter inch long, in short, close clusters. *Corolla*, short, cylindrical, and somewhat bell-shaped. *Calyx-teeth*, green and spreading. *Stamens*, hairy, not exserted from the corolla. May, June.

Leaves, three quarters to one inch long, oblong to lance-shape, stemless; smooth and shining above and beneath; finely and sharply bristle-toothed. *Stems* and *branches*, green and warty, and often with a hairy line running down each side.

Fruit, large, blue, sweet, ripening earlier than that of *V. vacillans*. July, August.

Found, growing in thick patches in dry, hard soil, from New Jersey to Illinois, and northward; very common in New England.

A bush six to fifteen inches high, the lowest and the earliest of the Blueberries.

A narrow-leaved lower variety *(var. angustifólium, G.)*, is found on the White Mountains of New Hampshire and far northward.

Var. nìgrum, Wood, has the leaves dark green, the berries black and shining.

V. Canadénse. *Kalm.*

This species differs from the preceding *(V. Pennsylvánicum)* chiefly in the following items:

Leaves, entire, downy beneath, and at least on the veins above. *Branchlets*, reddish-green and downy.

Found, from Maine and New Hampshire westward and northward.

Heath (Ericàceæ)

Low Blueberry. *V. vacillans, Solander.*

Flowering-branches, two to three inches or more in length, and without leaves, so that often much of the plant is leafless though covered with fruit.

Leaves, egg-shape to reverse egg-shape, edge entire or very finely toothed. *Branchlets*, yellowish-green, angular, and closely set with white dots.

Fruit, ripening later than that of *V. Pennsylvanicum*, August.

Found, in dry ground from New England westward and southward.

A bush one to two and one half feet high.

Fig. 74.—Common High Blueberry. Swamp Blueberry.
V. corymbòsum, L.

Flowers, in short clusters, appearing with or before the leaves. *Corolla*, more or less cylindrical, about one quarter to one third inch or more in length. *Stamens*, shorter than the corolla ("included"), hairy. *Style*, slightly exserted. May, June.

Leaves, variable in shape and size, mostly smooth, acute at each end, entire. *Branches*, green or purple. *Flowering-branches*, often almost leafless.

Fruit, large, blackish or purplish, slightly acid. August, September.

Found, in shady swamps and thickets from Canada to Florida.

A shrub five to ten feet high. It furnishes the late blueberry of the markets. A very variable species.

A marked variety *(var. atrocòcum, G.)* has the under surface of the leaves, even when old, and the branchlets downy or woolly.

Heath (Ericaceæ)

Bog Bilberry. *V. uliginòsum*, L.

Flowers, axillary, drooping, single, or two to three together, nearly sessile. *Corolla*, short, four-cleft, urn-shape. *Stamens*, eight, smooth. *Anthers*, with a slender hook (awn) back of each of the two horns. June, July.

Leaves, one quarter to one third inch long, dull, reverse egg-shape to oblong, entire. *Apex*, rounded or pointed, crowded toward the ends of the branches.

Fruit, four-celled, deep-blue or black, oblong, sweet, crowned with the style.

Found, on the mountain summits of New England and New York, the shores of Lake Superior, and northward.

A low, spreading shrub, four inches to two feet high.

V. cæspitòsum, Michx; var. *cuneifolium*, Nutt; *V. myrtillòides*, Hook; and *V. ovalifòlium*, Smith, are forms of Bilberries with the blossoms solitary, nodding on short axillary stems, the parts of the flower in fives; stamens, ten; the leaves more or less toothed. They are found on the shores of Lake Superior and northward.

(3) Genus ANDRÓMEDA, L.

Named with reference to the story of Andromeda (see below).

Flowers, mostly white, in clusters. *Corolla*, rounded, five-toothed. *Calyx*, without bracts. *Stamens*, ten. *Anthers*, attached near the middle. *Anther-cells*, opening by a pore at the end. *Seed-case*, free from the calyx.

Heath (Ericàceæ) 165

Fig. 74.—Common High Blueberry.   (V. corymbòsum, L.)   (*a*) Flower-cluster.

Heath (Ericàceæ)

Leaves, simple, alternate, entire (or in *Privet Andrómeda, A. ligustrina*, sometimes fine-toothed).

Fruit, globular to egg-shape, five-celled, many-seeded ; a capsule.

Fig. 75.—**Marsh Andrómeda. Wild Rosemary.** *A. polifòlia, L.*

Flowers, nearly round, crowded in terminal drooping clusters. *Corolla*, about one quarter inch long, rose-tinted. *Calyx*, white, tipped with red. *Anther-cells*, each terminating in a slender ascending awn. *Flower-stems*, about one half an inch long, pearl-white, springing from pointed and hollowed bracts of the same color at their base. June.

Leaves, evergreen, very narrow to oblong lance-shape, one to three inches in length by one sixth to one quarter of an inch in width ; very smooth, edges rolled back, thick, dark-green above, whitish beneath.

Fruit, globular, five-celled, many-seeded. A capsule.

Found, in wet ground from New Jersey and Pennsylvania to Minnesota, and far northward.

A very interesting evergreen shrub, six inches to two feet high.

Linnæus, in his *Tour in Lapland*, describes this shrub and tells why he chose for it the poetical name of Andrómeda :

"*Andrómeda polifòlia* was now (June 12) in its highest beauty, decorating the marshy grounds in a most agreeable manner. The flowers are quite blood-red before

Fig. 75.—Marsh Andrómeda. (A. polifòlia, L.) (a) Blossom slightly enlarged.
Fig. 76.—Stagger-Bush. (A. mariàna, L.)

Heath (*Ericàceæ*)

they expand, but when full-grown the corolla is of a flesh-color. . . . As I contemplated it, I could not help thinking of Andromeda as described by the poets; and the more I meditated upon their descriptions, the more applicable they seemed to the little plant before me. Andromeda is represented by them as a virgin of most exquisite and unrivalled charms. . . . This plant is always fixed on some little turfy hillock in the midst of the swamps, as Andromeda herself was chained to a rock in the sea, which bathed her feet as the fresh water does the roots of the plant. Dragons and venomous serpents surrounded her, as toads and other reptiles frequent the abode of her vegetable resembler. As the distressed virgin cast down her blushing face through excessive affliction, so does this rosy-colored flower hang its head, growing paler and paler until it withers away. . . . At length comes Perseus in the shape of summer, dries up the surrounding water, and destroys the monsters."

Fig. 76.—**Stagger-Bush.** *A. mariàna, L.*

Flowers, about five twelfths of an inch long, nodding in clusters on leafless branchlets. *Corolla*, somewhat egg-shape, white or pale red. *Calyx*, about two thirds as long as the corolla, parted nearly to the base. *Stamens*, two-toothed near the anthers, hairy, without awns. June and July.

Leaves, one to three inches long, smooth, oval, or oblong, acute at each end or sometimes with the apex rather blunted.

Fruit, egg-shape, with the narrowed end squared, as though cut off; five-celled, five-angled, many-seeded. *Seeds*, angular. A capsule. October.

Found, in dry places, in woods, etc., from Rhode Island and Pennsylvania southward.

A shrub two to three feet high, worthy of cultivation. Its common name is due to its reputation for poisoning young cattle.

Fig. 77.—Privet Andrómeda. *A. ligustrìna, Muhl.*

Flowers, scarcely one sixth of an inch long, downy, globular, white, crowded in terminal clusters; the clusters usually leafless, sometimes with two small leaflets at the base. *Flower-stems*, downy. *Anthers*, without awns. June, July.

Leaves, one to three inches long, entire or fine-toothed, more or less downy, reverse egg-shape and oval to lance-shape.

Fruit, globular, five-celled, five-angled, many-seeded; a capsule. September.

Found, in swampy ground from Canada southward. Common.

A shrub three to ten feet high.

(4) Genus Leucóthoë, Don.

Fig. 78.—Leucóthoë. *L. racemòsa (L.), Gray.*

Flowers, white, fragrant, with very short stems crowded in long, one-sided, usually erect spikes, mostly at the ends of the branches, each spike two to four inches long, with twelve to thirty downward-turned blossoms. *Corolla*, five-toothed, cylindrical or somewhat egg-shaped. *Calyx*, with two egg-shaped

Heath (Ericaceæ)

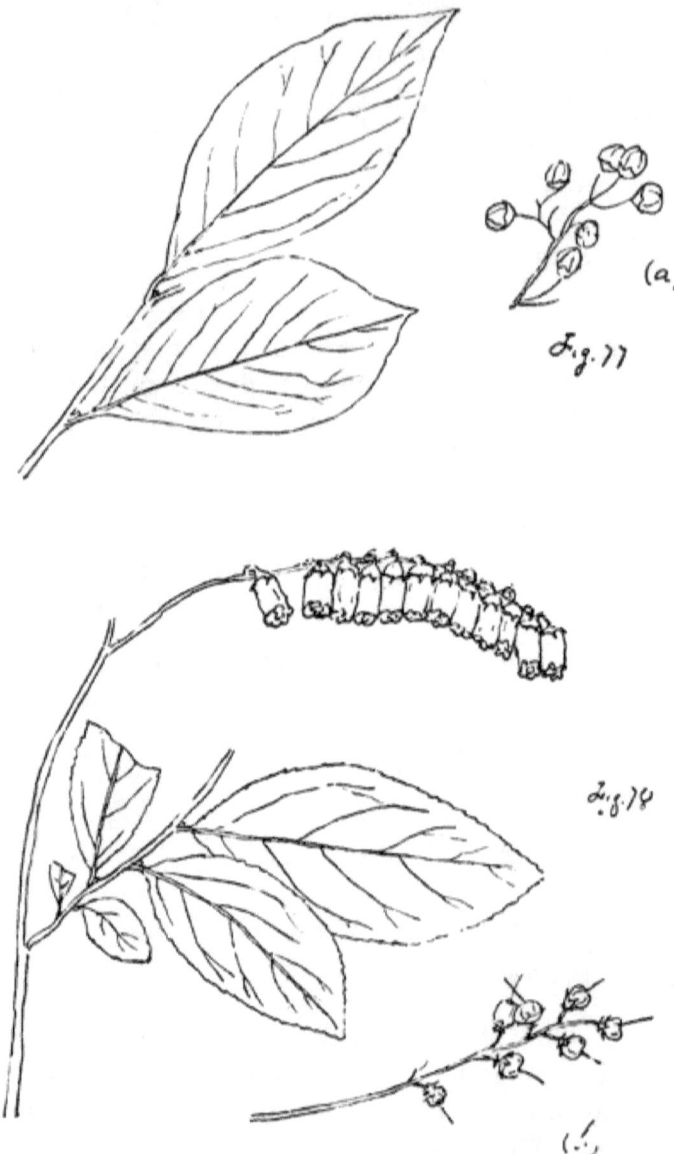

Fig. 77.—Privet Andrómeda. (A. ligustrina, Muhl.) (*a*) Fruit.
Fig. 78.—Leucóthoë. L. racemòsa (L.), **Gray**. (*b*) Fruit.

pointed, persistent *bracts* at base. *Stamens*, ten. *Anther-cells*, each with two awns at apex. *Seed-case*, free from the calyx. June, July.

Leaves, one to two and one half inches long, alternate, smooth, oblong to oval or reverse egg-shape, more or less pointed, fine-toothed. *Leaf-stem*, about one twelfth of an inch long.

Fruit, globular, depressed, five-celled, many-seeded, with the remains attached of the calyx and its two bracts and the long style. *Seeds*, angled not winged. A capsule.

Found, in moist woods and thickets from Canada to Florida, mostly near the coast.

A shrub four to ten feet high. The dry brown fruit-spikes of the previous year, with persistent calyx and bracts and style, often remain among the blossoms and green leaves of the new season. The plant is well worthy of cultivation.

(5) Genus CASSANDRA, Don.

Cassandra was a daughter of Priam and Hecuba.

Fig. 79.—Leather-Leaf. Cassandra. *C. calyculata (L.), Don.*

Flowers, white, with short stems, solitary in the axils of the twenty to thirty small upper leaves, so forming a long, one-sided leafy spike. *Corolla*, cylindrical, five-toothed. *Calyx*, with two persistent, egg-shaped bracts at its base. *Stamens*, ten. *Anther-cells*, each tapering into a beak that opens at its apex, without awns. *Seed-case*, free from the calyx. April, May.

Fig. 79.—Leather-Leaf. C. calyculàta (L.), Don.

Heath (*Ericaceæ*)

Leaves, about one inch long and half as wide (those of the flower-spikes smaller), oblong; blunt or slightly pointed; entire or very slightly toothed; shiny and dotted above, rusty beneath; mid-vein prominent, others scarcely noticeable.

Fruit, depressed, five-celled, many-seeded, with the covering of the seeds in two layers, the outer splitting at length into five parts, the inner into ten. *Seeds*, flattened, wingless. July.

Found, in wet places from Newfoundland to Minnesota, and southward to Georgia, often in large beds.

A nearly evergreen shrub two to four feet high.

Formerly Cassandra was included in the genus *Andromeda*. Inasmuch as Linnæus had given the latter name to the sweet little Lapland flower which he discovered—because it reminded him by its surroundings of the story of Andromeda chained in the midst of the waves—Don, when he rearranged the species chose the new name "Cassandra," to retain the classic suggestion.

(6) Genus KÁLMIA, L. (American Laurel.)

From the name of Peter Kalm, a pupil of Linnæus.

Flowers, showy, in clusters. *Corolla*, five-lobed, wheel- to bell-shaped, with ten pits for holding back the ten elastic stamens. *Calyx*, smaller than the ripened seed-case; persistent after the other parts of the flower have fallen. *Seed-case*, not adherent to the calyx.

Leaves, evergreen, opposite or alternate, entire, thick.

Fruit, mostly round, five-celled, many-seeded. A capsule.

Fig. 80.—Mountain Laurel. Calico-Bush. Spoon-Wood.
K. latifòlia, L.

Flowers, three quarters to five sixths of an inch across, rose-colored to white, in large, many-blossomed, terminal clusters, crowning the last year's leaves; sticky. May, June.

Leaves, mostly two to four inches long, oftenest alternate, sometimes opposite or in threes; shining, smooth on both sides. *Side-veins*, imperceptible below. *Bark*, in the larger specimens in short, rounded, and often flaky ridges, curiously forked at their ends. *Wood*, crooked, fine-grained, compact.

Fruit, rounded, five-celled, imperfectly five-angled, set with sticky hairs. September.

Found, usually in damp woods from Canada and Maine to Ohio and Kentucky, and in all the Atlantic States southward to Georgia.

One of our most beautifully flowering shrubs, evergreen, four to eight feet high, or sometimes even twenty feet in height, with crooked and twisting stems and branches. The leaves and juices are narcotic, and are said to be poisonous to browsing cattle. Well worthy of cultivation.

"When the clumps of Mountain Laurel are in bloom it is worth while going out of one's way to see them."

Heath (Ericàceæ)

Fig. 80.—Mountain Laurel. (K. latifòlia, L.)

Xenophon, in his *Retreat of the Ten Thousand*, tells how numbers of his warriors were poisoned through eating honey made by bees that had foraged among the abundant "laurel" flowers. The species may have been *Azalea Pontica*.

Fig. 81.—Sheep Laurel. Lambkill. *K. angustifolia*, L.

Flowers, about one half or two thirds smaller than those of the Mountain Laurel, closely resembling them, but of a deeper crimson and growing in small clusters at the sides of the branches in the axils of the last year's persistent leaves, and surmounted by the new leaves. May, July.

Leaves, one to two inches long, opposite in threes and in pairs, edge entire. *Apex* and *base*, slightly pointed or rounded; light green above, in winter often reddish-green or yellowish; below, whitish or pale. *Surfaces*, smooth. *Side-veins*, indistinct.

Fruit, rounded, depressed, five-celled, often clinging throughout the winter, its stems recurved. September.

Found, common, in rough fields and by ponds and marshes, from Canada to Carolina, and west to Kentucky, often in large patches.

A very pretty upright evergreen shrub one half to two feet or rarely four feet high. The leaves of this species also are said to be poisonous to cattle.

Pale Laurel. *K. glauca*, Ait.

Flowers, resembling in general the other laurel flowers, smooth, one half inch across, pale purple, in terminal clusters of eight to ten blossoms. *Flower-stems*, smooth. June.

Heath (Ericàceæ)

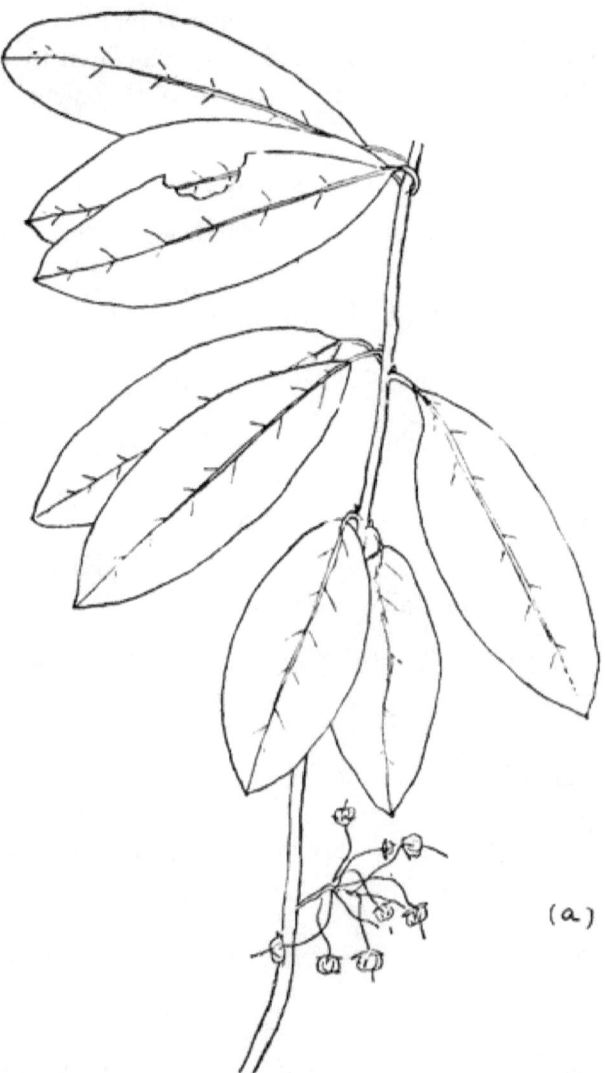

Fig. 81.—Sheep Laurel. (K. angustifòlia, L.) and fruit.

Heath (Ericaceæ)

Leaves, about one inch long, varying in width from scarcely one eighth to one half an inch, opposite, and often in threes, entire, with edge rolled back, nearly stemless. *Branchlets*, distinctly two-edged by ridges which extend from the bases of each pair of leaves to the pair below.

Fruit, somewhat egg-shape, smooth.

Found, mostly in swampy land from Kentucky and Pennsylvania far northward.

A straggling shrub, one to two feet high.

(7) Genus MENZIÈSIA, Smith.

Flowers, greenish-white or purplish, small, nodding in terminal clusters. *Corolla*, four-lobed. *Stamens*, eight. *Seed-case*, not adherent.

Leaves, alternate, reverse egg-shape. *Branchlets*, straggling, usually hairy and rusty.

Fruit, egg-shape, four-celled, many-seeded. A capsule.

The genus is represented by two species:

M. globélla, Gray, found from Minnesota Point, Lake Superior northwestward; and

M. globulàris, Salisb., found in the Alleghany Mountains from Pennsylvania southward.

(8) Genus RHODODÉNDRON, L. (Azaleas, etc.)

From a Greek word meaning "Rose-tree."

Flowers, showy, in terminal clusters. *Corolla*, deeply five-lobed (in *R. Rhodòra* two petals are wholly separate); often slightly irregular (or in *R. Rhodòra* very irregu-

Heath (Ericaceæ)

lar) ; bell or funnel-form. *Stamens*, twice as many as the petals, or of the same number (or in *R. nudiflorum*, five to seven). *Stamens* and *style* more or less exserted and declined, except in *R. maximum*. *Anther-cells*, opening by a round pore at the end. *Seed-case*, free from the calyx.

Leaves, chiefly alternate and entire.

Fruit, five-celled, many-seeded. *Seeds*, scale-like. A capsule.

Fig. 82.—Clammy Azalea. White Swamp Honeysuckle. Swamp Pink. *R. viscòsum (L.), Torr.*

Flowers, appearing after the leaves, white or rose-color, very fragrant, very sticky, in clusters of six to twelve blossoms. *Corolla*, downy, funnel-form ; tube about one inch long, nearly twice as long as the lobes. *Calyx*, minute. *Stamens*, five, slightly exserted from the tube. *Anthers*, nearly twice as long as in the Purple Azalea *(R. nudiflòrum)*. *Style*, much longer than the stamens. June, July.

Leaves, one to two inches long, alternate or in groups of five to six at the ends of the branchlets, reverse egg-shape to lance-shape, smooth, except at the delicately bristle-fringed margins and mid-vein. *Leaf-stem* and *branchlets*, bristly. *Apex*, often tipped with a brown, hard point.

Fruit, as above.

Found, in damp woods and swamps from Canada to Florida and Arkansas, mostly near the coast.

A shrub four to seven feet high. "Few flowers have been more valued and more frequently cultivated in European gardens than this."

Var. glaucum (Pursh.), G., found from New England to Virginia, has paler and sometimes rough-hairy leaves.

Var. nitidum (Lam.), G., found from the mountains of New York to Virginia, is a dwarf form with reverse-lanceolate leaves.

Smooth Azalea.   *R. arboréscens, Torr.*

Flowers, rose-color, very fragrant. *Corolla*, funnel-form, with the tube longer than the lobes; not at all or very slightly sticky. *Calyx*, conspicuous, as much as one sixth of an inch long, lobes oblong and acute. The five *stamens* and the *style* much exserted. *Scales* of the flower-buds large, yellowish-brown, and fringed. *Blossoms*, appearing after the leaves. May, July.

Leaves, very smooth on both sides, shiny above; the edges delicately bristle-fringed. *Branchlets*, smooth.

Fruit, as above.

Found, from the mountains of Pennsylvania to North Carolina.

A shrub ten to twenty feet high.

Fig. 83.—Purple Azalea. Pinxter-Flower.   *R. nudiflòrum (L.), Torr*

Flowers, one and one half inches across, very variable in color, white, pink, purple, buff, mottled; usually fragrant. *Corolla*, funnel-form. *Tube* (nearly one inch long), scarcely longer than the large lobes; downy, slightly sticky. *Calyx*, small and hairy.

181   Fig. 82.—Clammy Azalea.   R. viscòsum (L.), Torr.
Fig. 83.—Purple Azalea.   R. nudiflòrum (L.), Torr.   (a) Fruit.

Stamens, five to seven, twice as long as the tube, downy below the middle. *Style*, about three times as long as the tube. *Blossoms*, appearing with or before the leaves. April, May.

Leaves, reverse egg-shape to reverse lance-shape, downy beneath. *Young branchlets*, hairy, and often in whorls.

Fruit, as above. August.

Found, in woods and wet land from Canada to Florida and Texas; common, especially southward.

A crooked-stemmed, much branched shrub, with many varieties in cultivation.

Var. polyándra has ten to twenty stamens.

Flame-Colored Azalea. *R. calendulàceum, Torr.*

This species differs especially in the following items:

Flowers, one and one half to one and two thirds inches across, orange, changing to flame-color; abundant, covering the bush as the leaves are appearing; not fragrant, not sticky. *Corolla*, with its tube shorter than the lobes.

Found, from the mountains of Pennsylvania to Georgia.

It has many varieties in cultivation.

Fig. 84.—Rose Bay. Great Laurel. Rhododendron.
R. máximum, L.

Flowers, very showy, one to two inches broad, rose color or nearly white, sometimes dotted with yellow, in large clusters of fifteen to twenty blossoms at the ends of the branches. *Corolla*, bell-shaped, slightly irregular. The ten *stamens* and the *style* rarely exserted. *Flower-stem*, somewhat sticky. July, August.

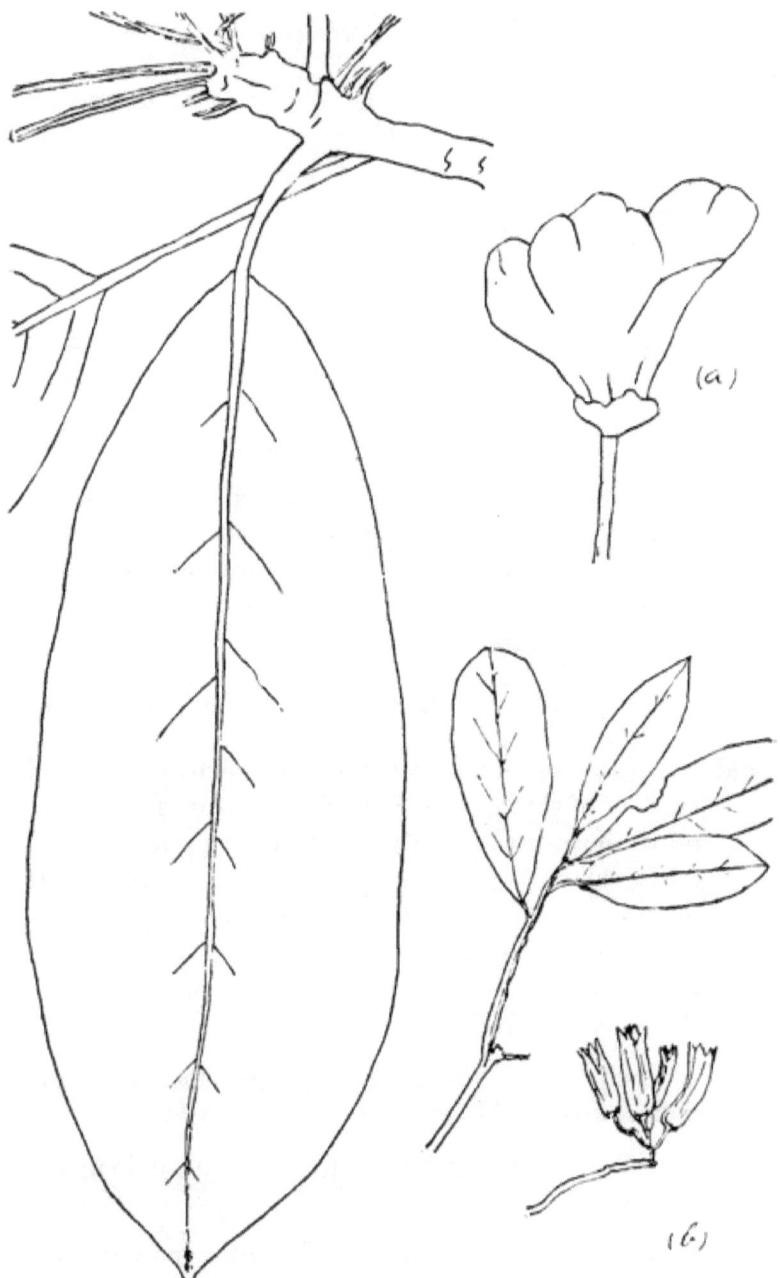

Fig. 84.—Great Laurel. (R. máximum, L.) (a) Flower.
Fig. 85.—Rhodòra. (R. Canadénse, B. S. P.) (b) Fruit.

Leaves, four to ten inches long, thick, alternate, mostly crowded at the ends of the branches, edge entire, dark and very smooth, and polished above, below paler, and often slightly rusty, the edges somewhat rolled.

Fruit, as above.

Found, not common in New England and New York; very common, especially along woody streams, in the mountains of Pennsylvania and southward. It is never found on limestone formations.

A magnificently flowering evergreen six to twenty feet high, with irregular, straggling branches, and hard and very fine-grained wood. It is the glory of the woods and glens where it appears. It is often cultivated, and easily, if it is sheltered from the sun.

Fig. 85.—Rhodòra. *R. Canadénse (L.), B.S.P., (R. Rhodòra, Don).*

Flowers, about one inch in length, irregular, in terminal clusters of three to five stemless blossoms. *Corolla*, purplish-rose, with scarcely any tube, split into two parts, the back part with three lobes, the front part of two nearly or quite distinct petals. *Calyx*, small, persistent. The ten unequal *stamens* and the *style* the length of the corolla. *Blossoms*, appearing before the leaves. April, May.

Leaves, oblong to somewhat reverse egg-shape, pale, more or less downy. *Bark*, smooth and brown.

Fruit, as above; oblong and downy. *Seeds*, oblong and winged.

Found, in moist ground from Canada to the mountains of Pennsylvania.

Heath (Ericàceæ)

A shrub one to three feet high, each stem divided into several branches; these, while still entirely leafless, bearing at their ends showy clusters of rosy blossoms.

I remember the first Rhodóra I ever saw; it was growing on a flat bit of land, close by the low bank of the Penobscot—a bush on fire, without a sign of green about it.

> "Rhodora! if the sages ask thee why
> This charm is wasted on the earth and sky,
> Tell them, dear, that if eyes were made for seeing,
> Then beauty is its own excuse for being.
> Why thou wert there, O rival of the rose!
> I never thought to ask, I never knew;
> But in my simple ignorance suppose
> The self-same power that brought me there brought you."
> RALPH WALDO EMERSON.

Lapland Rose Bay. *R. Lappónicum, Wahl.*

Flowers, violet-purple, dotted, about two thirds of an inch across, regular, in terminal, leafy clusters of few blossoms. *Corolla*, open, bell-shape. *Stamens*, five to ten, exserted. June, July.

Leaves, evergreen, thick, crowded, about one half an inch long and half as wide, elliptical, alternate; edge entire and revolute. *Apex*, blunt, roughened above and below with hollowed rusty scales. *Branches*, dotted, like the leaves, with rusty scales.

Found, on the high mountain summits of New England and New York, and northward to the Arctic coasts.

A thickly spreading evergreen shrub six to ten inches in height.

Heath (*Ericaceæ*)

(9) Genus LEDUM, L.

Fig. 86.—Labrador Tea. *L. latifolium*, Ait.

Flowers, white, small, in terminal clusters of about twelve or more blossoms. *Corolla*, of five separate petals, spreading and reverse egg-shape. *Calyx*, minute. *Stamens*, five to seven. *Anthers*, opening by terminal pores. *Seed-case*, not adherent to the calyx. May, July.

Leaves, one to two inches long, oblong or narrow-oblong, alternate, entire, margins strongly rolled, persistent; smooth above, very thickly covered beneath with a dense white or rusty wool.

Fruit, oblong, pointed, five-celled, many-seeded, splitting from the base upward; a capsule.

Found, in mountain woods and cold, damp ground from Pennsylvania to New England, westward and northward.

A shrub one to three feet high, easily recognized by its woolly-lined leaves. The leaves are very astringent, and have been used as a substitute for tea.

An introduced species found in Labrador and northwestward is *L. palustre, L.*, with narrower leaves, ten stamens, and shorter fruit.

Fig. 86.—Labrador Tea. (L. latifòlium, Ait.) (a) Fruit.

Heath (*Ericaceæ*)

(10) Genus CLÉTHRA, Gronov.

Fig. 87.—Sweet Pepper-Bush. White Alder. *C. alnifolia, L.*

Flowers, small, white, fragrant, in abundant terminal upright spikes from three to five inches in length. *Corolla* of five separate reverse egg-shaped petals. *Calyx*, whitish-downy, five-parted, persistent. *Stamens*, ten, usually exserted beyond the corolla. *Anthers*, arrow-shape. *Style*, slender, and three-cleft at the apex. *Flower-stems*, about one sixth of an inch long from the axil of a bract of about the same length, whitish-downy. *Seed-case*, not adherent to the calyx, but enclosed by it. July and August.

Leaves, two to about three or more inches long, alternate, edge-toothed, but entire toward the base, strongly straight-veined, mostly smooth, reverse egg-shape to oval with wedge-shaped base. *Leaf-stem*, short and downy.

Fruit, rounded, enclosed in the calyx, three-celled, many-seeded. *Seeds*, angular. A capsule.

Found, in swamps and low grounds from Eastern Canada to Georgia; most abundant near the coast.

A shrub three to eight feet high, often in large patches, filling the air with its heavy odor. Its fragrance and late blooming, as well as its showy flower-spikes, make it deserving of a place in the garden. Its clusters increase in size under cultivation. It is highly prized in England.

Heath (Ericàceæ)

Fig. 87.—Sweet Pepper-Bush. (C. alnifòlia, L.)

Olive (Oleàceæ)

24. Family OLEÀCEÆ.   (Olive Fam.)

Genus CHIONÀNTHUS, L.   (Fringe-Tree.)

From two Greek words meaning "snow" and "flowers."

Fig. 88.—Fringe-Tree.   Old Man's Beard. *C. Virgínica, L.*

Flowers, snow-white, in long, loose, drooping clusters. *Petals*, four, nearly an inch in length, very narrow, barely united at the base. *Calyx*, four-parted, very small, persistent. *Stamens*, two, very short. *Style*, one, notched. *Seed-case*, free from the calyx, two-celled, with four young seeds (only a part ripening). April, June.

Leaves, simple, opposite, three to six inches long, edges entire, smooth; outline oval to reverse egg-shape, very variable. *Apex*, pointed or sometimes rounded.

Fruit, one half to two thirds of an inch long, oval, purplish, one-celled, one- to three-seeded; a drupe.

Found, along streams from New Jersey and Southern Pennsylvania, southward.

A shrub six to ten feet high, or often a low tree; common in cultivation and very ornamental. The leaves are supposed to be useful as a tonic in fevers.

Olive (Oleaceæ)

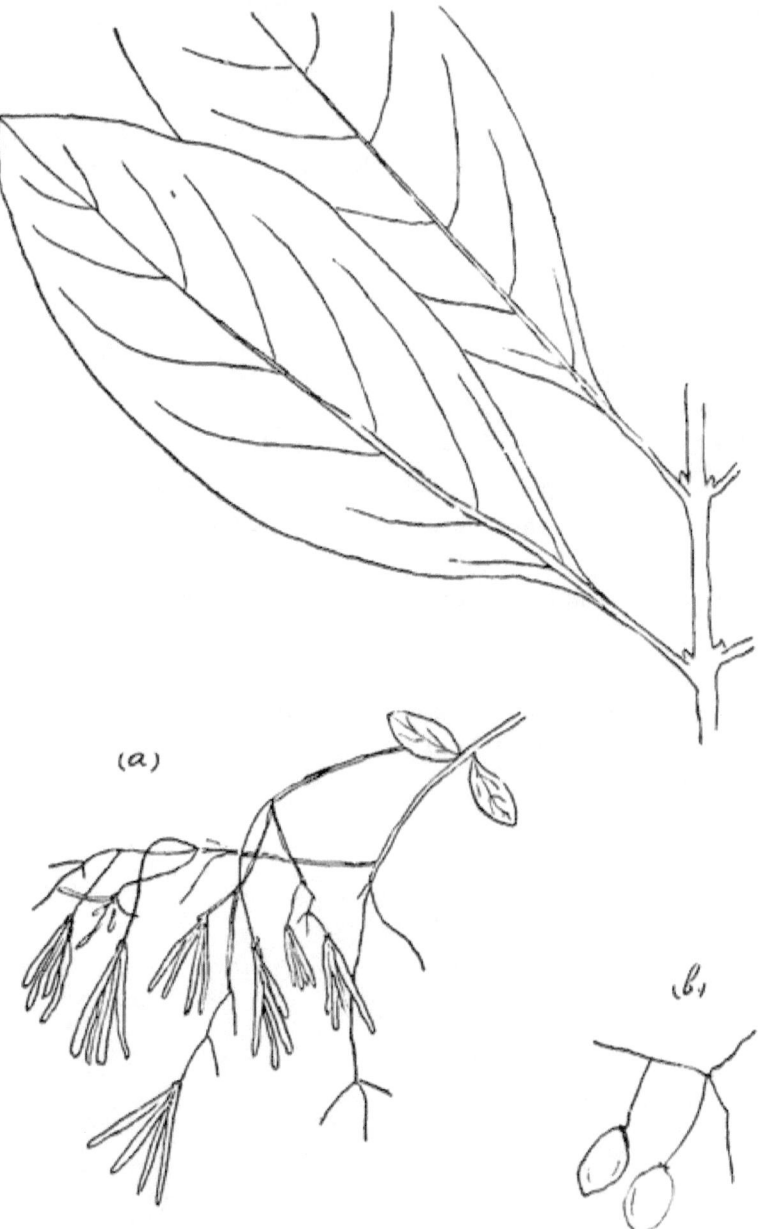

Fig. 88.—Fringe-Tree. (C. Virginica, L.) (a) Flower-cluster. (b) Fruit.

Olive (Oleàceæ)

Genus LIGÚSTRUM, Tourn.

Privet. [*L. vulgàre, L.*]

Flowers, small, white, close, in upright pyramid-shaped spikes at the ends of the branches. *Corolla*, four-lobed. *Calyx*, small, minutely four-toothed. *Stamens*, two. *Seed-case*, not adherent to the calyx. May, June.

Leaves, simple, three quarters to two inches long, opposite, edge entire, lance-shape and oval to reverse egg-shape, acute or blunt, very smooth, dark green.

Fruit, rounded, in cone-shaped bunches, two-celled, two- to four-seeded, black, bitter, ripe in July; a berry.

Found, in woods and thickets from New Jersey and New York to Virginia and westward.

A shrub four to eight feet high, naturalized from Europe. It is cultivated for ornament, and in the form of low hedges.

CLASS FIRST—Continued
(*Angiosperma*)

Division III
PETALS MOSTLY LACKING
(*Apetalous*)

25. Family LAURACEÆ. (Laurel Fam.)
Genus LÍNDERA, Thumb. (Spice-Bush.)
From the name of a Swedish botanist.

Fig. 89.—Spice-Bush. Fever-Bush. Benjamin-Bush. Wild Allspice. *L. Benzoin, Blume.*

Flowers, yellow, small, in almost stemless, lateral clusters, each cluster made up of several minor clusters of four to six flowers, with four early-falling scales at their base, appearing before the leaves. *Corolla*, lacking. *Calyx*, six-parted, the blossoms generally of two forms on different plants; the staminate with nine stamens in three rows, the inner lobed and with glands at their base; the pistillate with fifteen to eighteen undeveloped stamens in two forms. *Style*, one. *Seed-case*, round and not adherent to the calyx. March, April.

Leaves, two to four inches long, simple, alternate, entire, wedge-shape to reverse egg-shape and oval, nearly smooth.

Fruit, red, reverse egg-shape, one-celled, one-seeded; a drupe.

Found, from Ontario and New England southward in damp woods.

An aromatic shrub six to fifteen feet high. The powdered berries have sometimes been used as a substitute for allspice, and the leaves for tea.

Laurel (Lauraceæ) 195

Fig. 89.—Spice-Bush. (L. Benzòin, Blume.) (a) Flower clusters.

Dáphne (Thymeæàceæ)

26. Family THYMELÆACEÆ. (Dáphne Fam.)

Genus DÍRCA, L. (Leatherwood.)

Fig. 90.—Leatherwood. Moosewood. *D. palústris, L.*

Flowers, light yellow, three or four in a cluster at the sides of the branches, appearing before the leaves. *Corolla*, wanting. *Calyx*, tubular, without spreading lobes, its edge wavy or slightly four-toothed. *Stamens*, eight, long and slender, alternating in length. *Style*, one, it and the stamens exserted. *Seed-case*, not attached to the calyx, one-celled, one-seeded. April.

Leaves, three to four inches long, simple, alternate, entire, reverse egg-shape to oval. *Apex*, pointed or blunt. *Base*, sometimes slightly heart-shaped. *Leaf-stem*, short, and covering the leaf-bud at its base. *Bark*, fibrous, and remarkably tough.

Fruit, about one half an inch long, oval, pointed, reddish, one-celled, one-seeded; a berry-like drupe.

Found, in damp woods from Canada to the Gulf.

A much branching shrub, two to five feet high, with white wood, with bark that is leather-like in its toughness. "It has so great strength that a man cannot pull apart so much as covers a branch one half or one third of an inch in diameter." Millers and others use it for thongs, and from the pliant branches baskets are made. The Indians used it for cordage.

Dáphne (Thymelæaceæ)

Fig. 90.—Leatherwood. (D. palústris, L.)
Fig. 91.—Shepherdia. (S. Canadénsis, Nutt.)

Genus DÁPHNE, L. (Mezèreum.)

Mezèreum. Dáphne. [*D. mezèreum, L.*]

This species differs from the above chiefly in the following items:

Calyx, purplish-rose, rarely white, with four spreading lobes. *Stamens* and *style*, if present, not exserted.

Leaves, lance-shape.

Found, escaped from cultivation in Canada, New York, and Massachusetts. Introduced from Europe.

27. Family ELÆAGNÁCEÆ. (Oleaster Fam.)

Genus SHEPHÉRDIA, Nutt. (Shepherdia.)

Fig. 91.—**Shepherdia.** *S. Canadensis, Nutt.*

Flowers, very small, yellowish, nearly stemless, of two kinds on the same bush. *Corolla*, wanting. *Calyx*, four-parted. The *staminate flowers* with eight stamens, in lateral clusters; the *pistillate* often solitary, with one *style*, and with a one-seeded *seed-case* enclosed by, but not adherent to, the calyx.

Leaves, one to two inches long, opposite, entire, oblong or egg-shape, beneath very white-downy and sprinkled thickly with rusty scales. *Branchlets*, and *flowers*, also marked with rusty scales.

Fruit, size of a small pea, round or oval, yellowish-red, pulpy, sweetish, but not edible, one-celled, one-seeded, berry-like; really an akene within the pulpy calyx.

Found, from New York and Vermont westward and northward.

A shrub three to six feet high, curious and ornamental.

28. Family LORANTHACEÆ. (Mistletoe Fam.)

Genus PHORADÉNDRON, Nutt. (Am. Mistletoe.)

From two Greek words meaning "thief" and "tree," because of the mistletoe's parasitical growth.

Fig. 92.—American Mistletoe. *P. flavescens*, *Nutt.*

Flowers, small, whitish, in spikes in the angles of the leaves, of two kinds, on separate plants. *Corolla*, wanting. *Calyx*, usually three-lobed. The *staminate flowers* with a sessile anther at the base of each lobe; the *pistillate* with a *seed-case* that is one-celled, one-seeded, and adherent to the calyx.

Leaves, three quarters to one and a third inches in length, simple, opposite, entire, reverse egg-shape to oval. *Base*, slightly pointed or rounded, stemless, thick, fleshy, with three strong veins radiating from the base. *Stem*, brittle at the joints.

Fruit, round, white, the size of a small pea, in spikes and clusters, one-seeded; pulpy, the pulp very sticky; a berry.

Found, from New Jersey to Southern Indiana and southward, growing firmly on the branches of various trees.

A much-branching evergreen parasite, one to one and a half feet high. Its propagation is by help of the sticky pulp, which holds the fruit to the bark where it falls, until the seed takes root. As the plant grows it feeds on the juices of the tree.

In Scandinavian mythology it is recorded that Balder (the Scandinavian counterpart of Apollo) was proof

Sandalwood (Santalàceæ)

against anything whatsoever that had its source in either of the four elements, fire, air, earth, or water. But his enemy Loke, the Spirit of Evil, made an arrow out of mistletoe, which grows from none of these things, and with this arrow Balder was slain.

The Druids held in the highest veneration whatever grew on the oak; especially they reverenced the mistletoe. When it was found, two fat bulls were sacrificed beneath it, and a priest, clothed in white, cut it down with a golden knife.

Traces of the ancient esteem for the mistletoe are still found in old English and German customs, such as "kissing under the mistletoe," and its various uses at the Christmas-time. Its sprays were supposed to have magical powers; they were used as charms.

There is a tradition that the cross was made from the wood of the mistletoe, which up to that time was a large tree, but then was condemned to live for evermore as a parasite.

29. Family SANTALÀCEÆ. (Sandalwood Fam.)

Genus PYRULÀRIA, Michx. (Oil-Nut.)

<small>From a Latin word meaning "pear," because of the shape of its fruit.</small>

Fig. 93.—Oil-Nut. Buffalo-Nut. *P. pùbera, Michx.*

Flowers, small, greenish, in short, terminal, few-flowered spikes. *Corolla*, wanting. *Calyx*, five-cleft, sometimes of two kinds on separate plants. *Staminate flowers*, with five stamens opposite the sepals; *pistillate* with the one *style* short and thick, and the *seed-case* adherent to the calyx, excepting at its flat summit, one-celled, and two- to four-seeded. May.

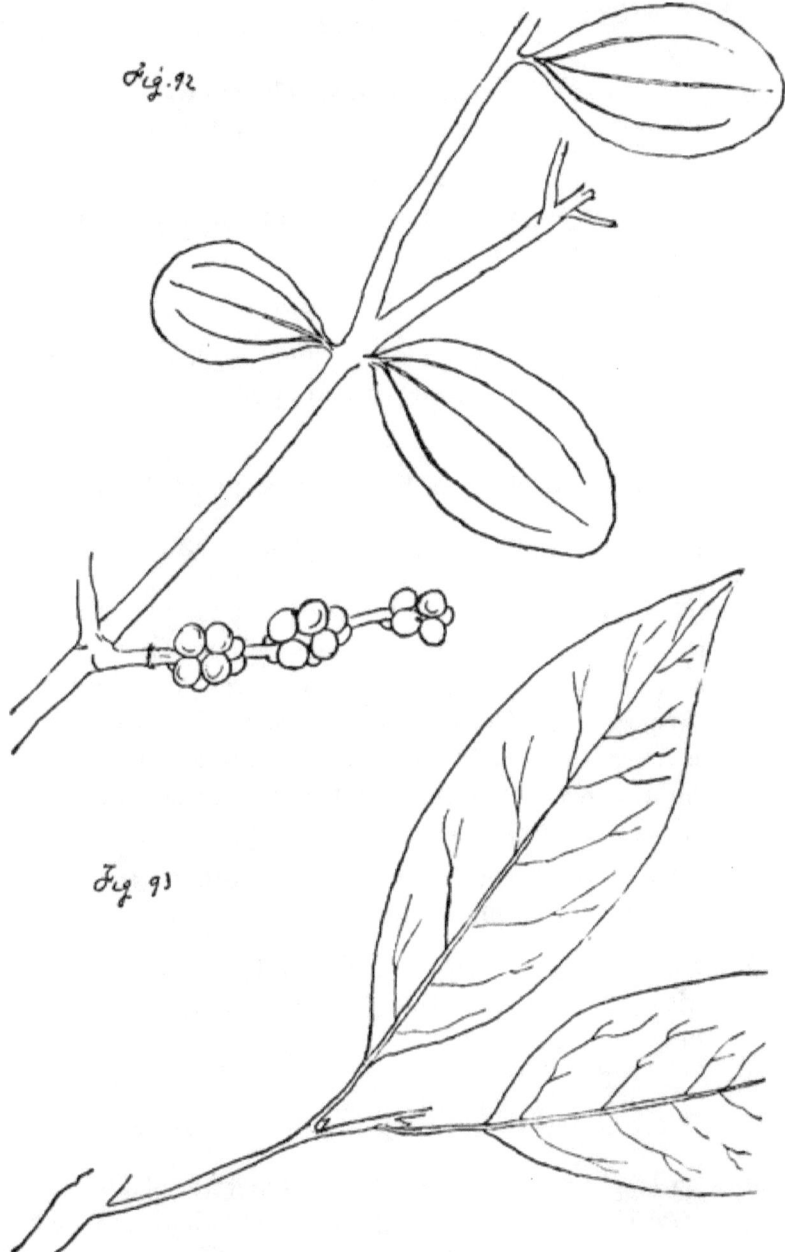

Fig. 92.—American Mistletoe. (P. flavéscens, Nutt.)
Fig. 93.—Oil-Nut. (P. pùbera, Michx.)

Sweet-Gale (*Myricaceæ*)

Leaves, two to three inches long, simple, alternate, entire, oblong to egg-shape, very veiny, minutely dotted.

Fruit, about one inch long, pear-shaped, fleshy, crowned with the remains of the persistent calyx, one-celled, one-seeded; drupe-like.

Found, from the mountains of Pennsylvania to Georgia.

A shrub three to twelve feet high, with every part, especially the fruit, flavored with an acrid oil.

30. Family MYRICACEÆ. (Sweet-Gale Fam.)

Genus MYRICA, L. (Bayberry, etc.)

Flowers, solitary, under a scale-like bract, of two kinds: the *staminate* in oblong or cylindrical clusters; the *pistillate* axillary, in egg-shape, oval, or globular clusters. *Corolla*, lacking. *Stamens*, two to eight, somewhat united below. *Seed-case*, free, with two to eight scales at its base, and two thread-like stigmas, one-celled, one-seeded.

Leaves, simple, alternate, entire or toothed, fragrant, resinous-dotted under the lens.

Fruit, one-celled, one-seeded, round to oblong, coated with wax or with resinous grains; a dry, drupe-like nut.

Fig. 94.—Bayberry. Wax Myrtle. *M. cerifera*, L.

Flowers, the two kinds mostly on separate plants, the *staminate* clusters oblong, erect, less than one inch long, on the sides of the last year's twigs, scattered; the *pistillate* clusters oval. May.

Fig. 94.—Bayberry. (M. cerifera, L.)
Fig. 95.—Sweet-Gale. (M. Gàle, L.)
Fig. 96.—Sweet Fern. M. asplenifòlia (L.) Banks.

Sweet-Gale (*Myricaceæ*)

Leaves, one and one half to three inches long, smooth, and shining on both sides. *Apex*, pointed or blunt, and tipped with the end of the mid-vein, entire or remotely toothed toward the apex. *Leaf-stem*, distinct.

Fruit, about one eighth inch in diameter, round and nut-like, greenish at first, then blackish, and when ripe crusted with whitish wax, clustered on short stems below the leaves, usually four to nine in a cluster, sometimes remaining in place for two or three years.

Found, near the coast from Nova Scotia to Florida, and on Lake Erie, oftenest on dry, sandy soil.

A compact, much-branching shrub, two to eight feet high, often growing in masses. The wax of the gathered berries, when removed by soaking in boiling water, forms the "bayberry tallow" of commerce.

"The production of myrica wax, or bayberry tallow, has been carried on to a somewhat large extent, mostly for the manufacture of candles and soap. Candles made from this wax, though quite brittle, are less greasy than others, are slightly aromatic, and are smokeless after snuffing. The wax is obtained by boiling the berries and then skimming the water. It saponifies readily with a solution of caustic potash, yielding a fragrant soap. Four pounds of berries yield about one pound of wax.

Fig. 95.—Sweet-Gale. Dutch Myrtle. *M. Gale, L.*

Flowers, the two kinds mostly on separate plants; the *staminate* clusters terminal, one inch or more in length, closely clustered; the *pistillate* clusters axillary, about one eighth of an inch in length, oval.

Sweet-Gale (Myricaceæ)

Leaves, three quarters to one and one half inches long, entire for about two thirds the length, sharp-toothed toward the apex, fragrant when crushed, appearing later than the flowers. *Apex*, blunt or slightly pointed. *Leaf-stem*, very short.

Fruit, round, dotted; two-winged by two thick, egg-shaped scales, crowded in an oblong head; usually two to six nuts in each cluster.

Found, on the borders of ponds from Canada and southward in the mountains, to Carolina.

A branching shrub, three to five feet high.

 Fig. 96.—Sweet-Fern. *M. asplenifolia (L.), Banks.*

Flowers, the two kinds often on the same plant, the pistillate forms in rounded clusters with the seed-cases surrounded by eight narrow, persistent scales. April, May.

Leaves, one to six inches long, narrow, pointed, with large rounded, lobe-like teeth.

Fruit, a small nut, egg-shape or oval, brown, in clusters, and clothed with the lengthened persistent scales. September.

Found, in dry, poor, ground, often in large patches, from North Carolina northward and westward.

 A shrub, round-headed, one to two feet high, very aromatic when crushed. It is much used in some localities, medicinally, for summer complaints and for bathing bruises, and in rheumatism.

 "The early colonists of Massachusetts, unfamiliar with the innocent qualities of the plant, tell how, in a journey through the 'wilderness' from Boston to Concord, some of their number were made to faint by the powerful odor of the abundant sweet fern, growing in large patches along their way."—RALPH WALDO EMERSON in *Atlantic Monthly* of January, 1892.

31. Family CUPULÍFERÆ. (Oak Fam.)

Flowers, of two kinds on the same plant: the *staminate* forms in long, slim clusters (or in the beech, in rounded clusters); the *pistillate*, variously arranged. *Seed-cases*, two- to seven-celled, with one to two young seeds in each cell, but all disappearing in fruit excepting one cell and one seed.

Leaves, simple, alternate, toothed or lobed.

Fruit, one-celled, one-seeded; clustered nutlets, or nuts, or acorns.

GUIDE TO THE GENERA.

(1) Bétula (Birch).   (2) Álnus (Alder).   (3) Córylus (Hazel-nut).
(4) Carpinus (Hornbeam). (5) Quércus (Oak).   (6) Castánea (Chestnut).

(1) Genus BÉTULA, Tourn. (Birch.)

Flowers, the *staminate* forms in long, drooping, stemless clusters, golden in spring, appearing with or before the leaves, three blossoms and two small bracts to each shield-like scale; the *pistillate* forms in oblong or cylindrical stemmed clusters, two or three blossoms to each three-lobed bract.

Leaves, simple, alternate, toothed.

Fruit, clustered, broadly winged, scale-like, crowned with the two stigmas; a scale-like nutlet.

Fig. 97.—Low Birch. *B. pùmila, L.*

Flowers, the *pistillate* forms in short, erect clusters; clusters of both forms about one half to three quarters of an inch long.

Oak (Cupuliferæ)

Fig. 97.—Low Birch. (B. pùmila, L.) (*a*) Fruiting cluster.

Leaves, one half to one and one third inches long, rounded or wedge-shape, or sometimes egg-shape. *Bark*, brownish.

Fruit, with its wing mostly narrower than the rest of the nutlet.

Found, in wet ground in Connecticut and New Jersey, and westward, and in the mountains of New England and northward.

A shrub two to eight feet high.

Dwarf Birch. *B. glandulosa, Michx.*

Flower-clusters and *fruit*, much as in the last.

Leaves, reverse egg-shape to rounded, one half to three quarters of an inch long.

Branches, marked with resinous, wart-like dots.

Found, from the mountains of New England far northward.

A shrub one to four feet high.

B. papyrifera, var. minor, Tuck., is a low form of the "Paper Birch," six to nine feet high, found in the higher parts of the White Mountains.

Oak (Cupuliferæ)

(2) Genus ÁLNUS, Tourn. (Alder.)

Staminate flowers, in long, drooping clusters with three (sometimes six) blossoms, and four or five small bracts to each shield-shaped scale. *Pistillate flowers*, in oval or oblong clusters, with two or three blossoms to each fleshy scale. *Scales* and *bracts*, woody in fruit.

Leaves, simple, alternate, toothed.

Fruit, in "cones," sometimes winged, scale-like, clustered. A scale-like nutlet.

Green Alder. Mountain Alder. *A. viridis, D. C.*

Pistillate clusters, one half to two thirds of an inch long, on slender stalk, appearing with the leaves. April.

Leaves, two to four inches long, egg-shape to rounded and heart-shaped.

Fruit, with a thin, broad wing. August.

Found, along streams in the Alleghany Mountains to North Carolina, and from Western Massachusetts and New York westward and far northward.

A shrub three to eight feet high.

Oak (Cupuliferæ)

Fig. 98.—Smooth Alder. *A. serrulàta, Willd.*

Flowers, appearing before the leaves; the staminate clusters two to three inches in length, forming drooping tassels of purple and gold, three to five together on short terminal foot-stalks; the fertile clusters usually from the same point, erect, three or four together, one quarter to one third of an inch long, but later enlarging to one third to one half inch long, and becoming hard and cone-like. March, April.

Leaves, two to four inches long, often crumpled between the prominent veins, oval to reverse egg-shape. *Base*, acute or rounded, green above and below, sharp-toothed, sometimes double-toothed, mostly smooth, usually slightly downy on the veins beneath.

Fruit, wingless, egg-shape. September.

Found, common in wet land from Massachusetts westward and southward.

A shrub six to fifteen feet high, often forming thick clumps, the common alder southward. The wood, when large enough, is excellent for fuel. The charcoal from it is preferred to any other in compounding gunpowder.

Speckled Alder. Hoary Alder. *A. incàna, Willd.*

Flowers, with much the same aspect as those of the smooth alder.

Leaves, two to four inches long, egg-shape to broad oval. *Base*, rounded or slightly heart-shaped, or sometimes pointed, mostly downy and hairy beneath, sharp-toothed, sometimes double-toothed.

Oak (Cupuliferæ)

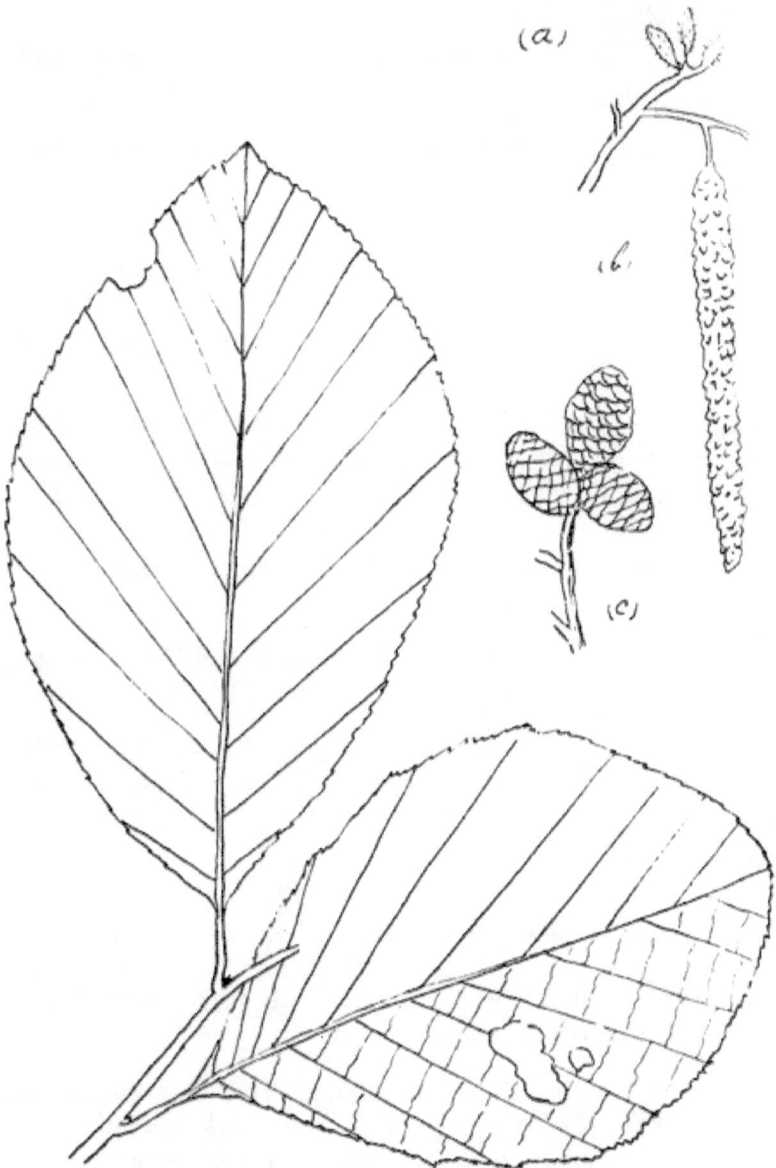

Fig. 98.—Smooth Alder. (A. serulàta, Willd.)
(a) Pistillate clusters. (b) Staminate clusters. (c) "Cones."

Oak (Cupuliferæ)

Fruit, wingless, slightly margined, orbicular.

Found, in wet land from Massachusetts westward and northward.

A shrub eight to twenty feet high; the common alder northward.

(3) Genus CÓRYLUS, Tourn. (Hazel-nut.)

<small>Probably from a Greek word meaning "helmet" from the bonnet-like covering of the nut.</small>

Flowers, appearing before the leaves, the staminate forms with eight *stamens*, in long, drooping clusters; the pistillate form, several from a scaly bud, each a single adherent *seed-case* tipped with the end of the calyx, with two side bractlets, a style, and two slender stigmas. April.

Leaves, simple, alternate, toothed, folded lengthwise in the bud.

Fruit, the size of a small marble, oval or rounded to oblong, bony, covered with a large, leafy, downy wrap with slashed edges, often in clusters; a bony nut.

Fig. 99.—**Wild Hazel-nut.** *C. Americàna, Walt.*

Flowers, the staminate clusters two to three inches long, and two to five together. April.

Leaves, three to six inches long, rather coarse, rough above, downy and hairy on the veins beneath, outline variable from egg-shape to slightly reverse egg-shape. *Leaf-stem*, covered with glandular hairs.

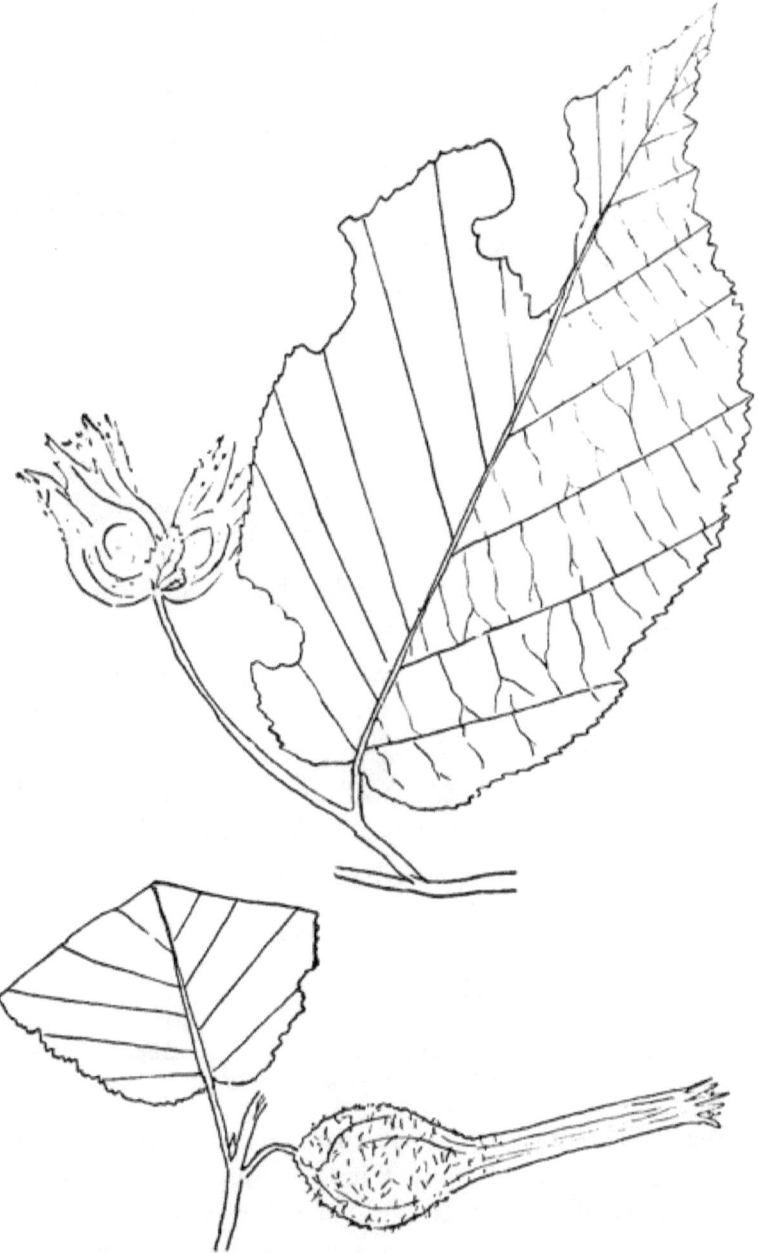

Fig. 99.—Hazel-nut. (C. Americàna, Walt.)
Fig. 100.—Beaked Hazel-nut. (C. rostràta, Ait.)

Fruit, rounded, the wrap about twice the length of the nut, broad, with spreading and coarsely-toothed edge, opening down to the nut. September.

Found, common, often forming clumps along the borders of fields and woods from Canada southward.

A shrub four to eight feet high. Its nuts are of pleasant flavor, but inferior in quality to the English "filberts."

Fig. 100.—**Beaked Hazel-nut.** *C. rostràta, Ait.*

Flowers, the staminate clusters about one inch long, alone or in pairs. April.

Leaves, much as in the preceding, but oftenest smaller— about three inches or less in length.

Fruit, much as in the preceding, but with the wrap curiously lengthened into a long, tubular beak. September.

Found, from Nova Scotia to New Jersey and westward, and in the mountains southward to Georgia.

A shrub two to six feet high, much less common than the preceding.

(4) Genus CARPÌNUS, L.

Fig. 101.—**Hornbeam. Ironwood. Water Beech. Blue Beech.** *C. Caroliniàna, Walt.*

Flowers, the staminate form with several *stamens* in the axil of a scale-like bract, in drooping clusters an inch, or usually less, in length at the sides of the branches; the pistillate form in numerous pairs, spiked in a loose, terminal cluster, about two inches long. April.

Oak (Cupuliferæ)

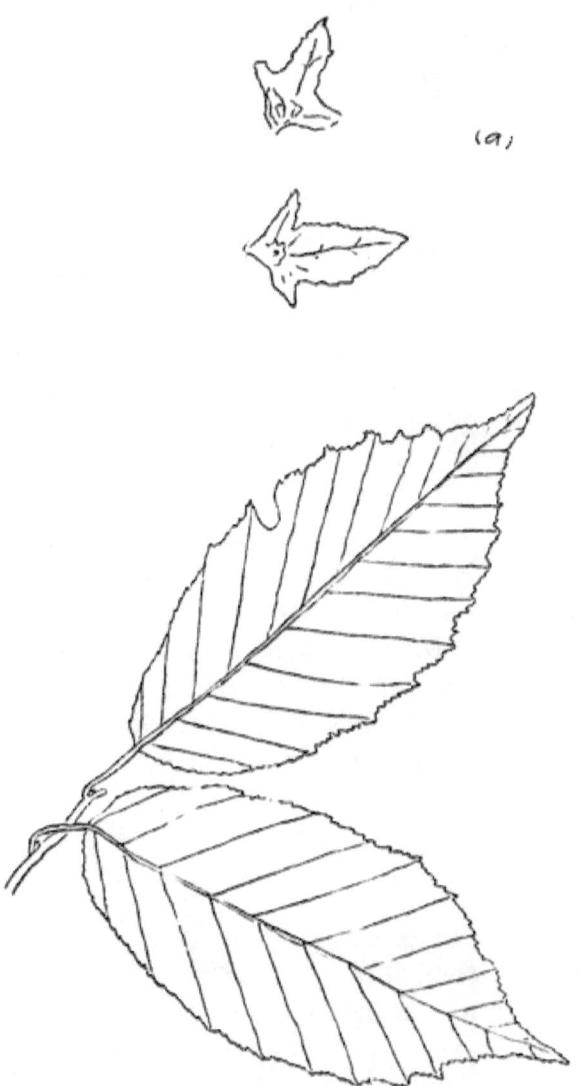

Fig. 101.—Hornbeam. (C. Caroliniàna, Walt.) (a) Fruit scales.

Oak (Cupuliferæ)

Leaves, usually three or four inches long, but with many smaller leaves of varying size on the same branch; nearly smooth, slightly hairy on the straight and distinct ribs, and in their angles.

Fruit, in a loose, drooping cluster, with leaf-like, strongly three-lobed scales; dark, small, egg-shape, placed in pairs base to base; clustered nutlets. October.

Found, along streams and in swamps; quite common north, south, and west; southward often as a tree.

A shrub (or sometimes a small tree) usually ten to twenty feet high, but in the southern Alleghany Mountains sometimes reaching a height of fifty feet. Its wood is white, very compact, and strong.

(5) Genus Quércus, L.

Flowers, small, greenish or yellowish, the staminate form with a two- to eight-lobed calyx, and with three to twelve stamens, in slender, drooping clusters; the pistillate form with a *seed-case* containing three more or less complete cells, and six young seeds (only one of which develops), and with a three-lobed stigma—all in a scaly, bud-like wrap, which becomes the cup of the acorn.

Leaves, simple, alternate.

Fruit, an acorn.

Fig. 102.—**Dwarf Chestnut Oak. Scrub-Oak.** *Q. Muhlenbérgii, Eng. var. humilis, Britton. (Q. prinoides, Willd.).*

Leaves, three to four inches long, with large, or sometimes small wavy teeth, usually four to eight on each side, light green and polished above, whitish or bluish, and fine downy beneath. *Leaf-stem,* one quarter to three quarters of an inch long.

Oak (Cupuliferæ)

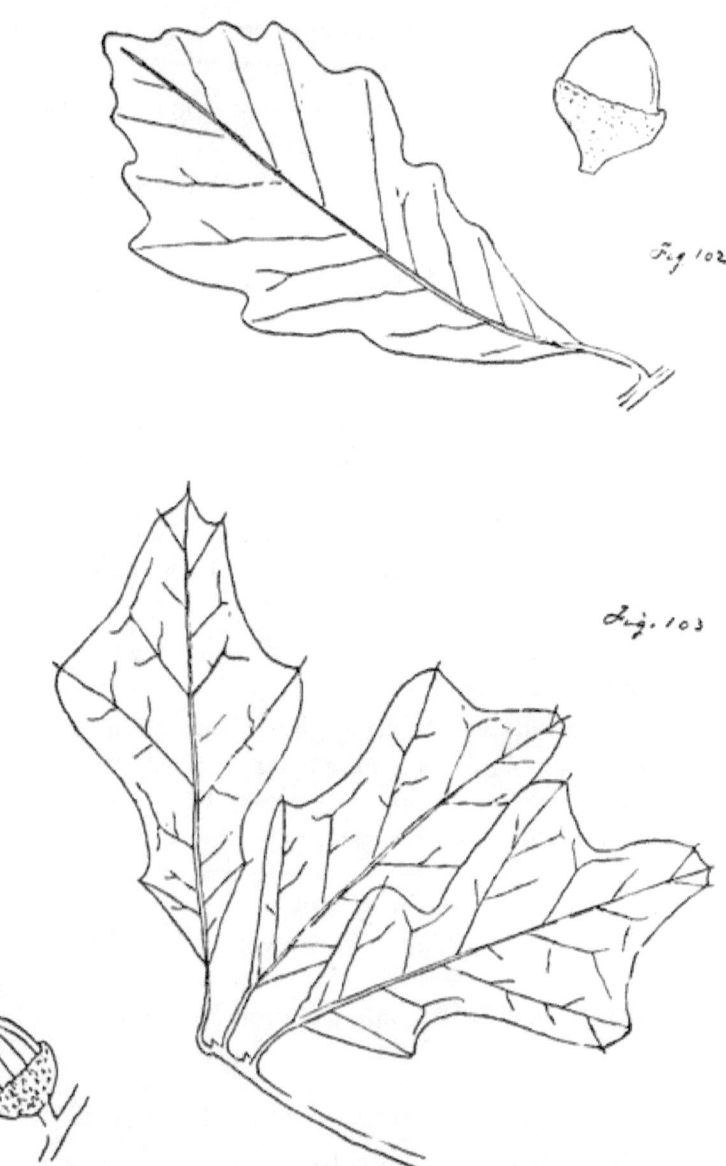

Fig. 102.—Dwarf Chestnut Oak. (Q. Muhlinbérgii, Eng. var. hùmilis, Britton.)
Fig. 103.—Bear Oak. (Q. ilicifòlia, Willd.)

Fruit, middle size, abundant, sweet, egg-shape. *Cup*, rounded, with small scales. September.

Found, from Massachusetts westward and southward; not common.

A shrub seldom, if ever, more than three or four feet in height; one of the smallest of the oaks.

Fig. 103.--Bear Oak. Shrub Oak. Scrub-Oak. *Q. ilicifolia, Willd.*

Leaves, two to four inches long, with three to seven (usually five) angular, often bristle-tipped lobes, beneath downy, especially in the axils of the veins, and very silvery or grayish-white. *Leaf-stem* very variable in length.

Fruit, abundant, oval or egg-shape, about one half inch long, dark brown, marked lengthwise with pale lines. *Cup*, saucer-shape with a top-shaped base. September.

Found, on barren and sandy soil from New England southward; common.

A much branching, straggling shrub three to eight feet high, often growing in masses; called "bear oak," possibly from the liking of bears, when bears were common, for the abundant acorns.

FROM NOTE-BOOK.

February. Bear Oak. The silver-backed, little brown leaves still cling thickly to the crowded and scraggy branches. Most of the many acorns have fallen; a few cups remain in place.

(6) Genus CASTANEA, Tourn. (Chestnut.)

Fig. 104.—Dwarf Chestnut. Chinquapin. *C. pumila, Mill.*

Flowers, yellowish-white, appearing later than the leaves. *Calyx*, mostly six-lobed; the staminate with eight

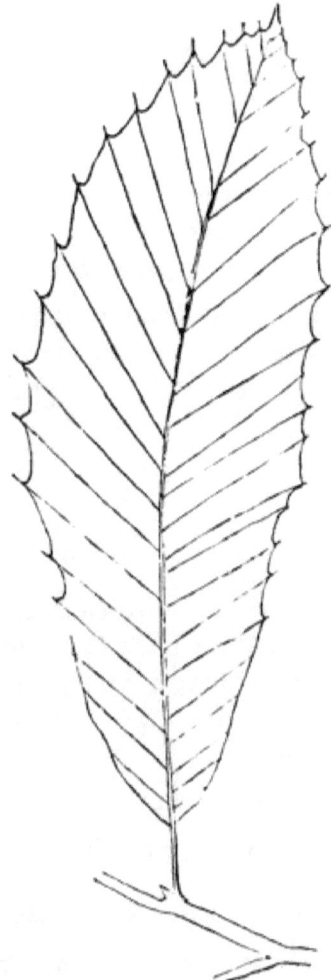

Fig. 104.—Dwarf Chestnut. (C. pùmila, Mill.)

to twenty *stamens*, in drooping clusters two to three inches long; the pistillate, usually three together, in an oval, scaly, prickly wrap.

Leaves, three to five inches long, sharp-toothed, prominently straight-veined, white-downy beneath. *Base*, usually blunt.

Fruit, solitary, oval, pointed, about one half the size of the common chestnut, very sweet, not flattened, enclosed in a very prickly wrap about one and a half inches in diameter; a prickly-covered nut. October.

Found, from New Jersey and Southern Pennsylvania south to Florida and west to Indiana and Texas.

A spreading shrub (or sometimes a small tree) six to twelve feet high.

32. Family SALICACEÆ.

Genus SALIX, Tourn. (Willow.)

Flowers, in long clusters, one flower to each entire-edged bract; the staminate and pistillate forms on separate plants; the staminate with two to ten (mostly two) *stamens;* the pistillate with *style* short or wanting, and two short stigmas.

Leaves, alternate, usually long, narrow, and pointed.

Fruit, one-celled, many-seeded; a capsule.

Fig. 105.—Long-leaved Willow. *S. longifolia, Muhl.*

Leaves, very narrow-lanceolate, two to four inches long, tapering at each end, remotely sharp-toothed, nearly stemless.

Found, growing in thick clumps along the coast from Maine to the Potomac; not common.

Willow (Salicàceæ)

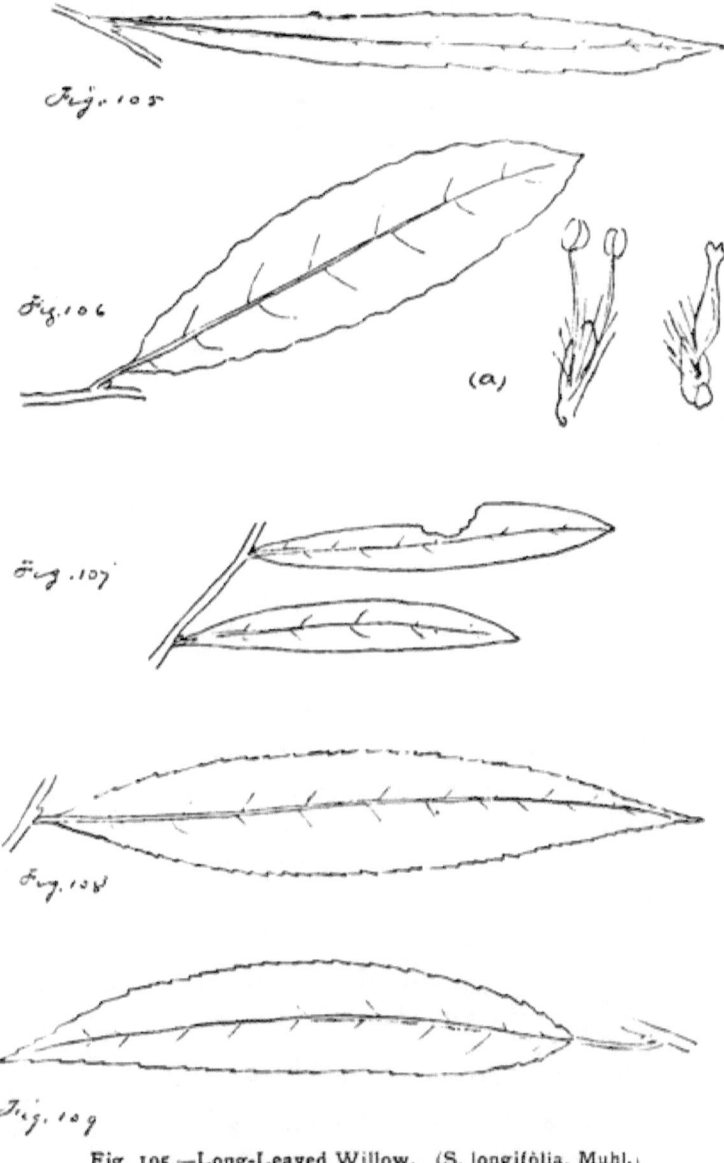

Fig. 105.—Long-Leaved Willow. (S. longifòlia, Muhl.)
Fig. 106.—Prairie Willow. (S. hùmilis, Marsh.)
(a) Staminate and pistillate flowers enlarged.
Fig. 107.—Dwarf Gray Willow. (S. tristis, Ait.)
Fig. 108.—Silky Willow. (S. sericea, Marsh.)
Fig. 109.—Long-Stalked Green Osier. (S. petiolàris, Smith.)

Willow (Salicàceæ)

A peculiar American species, about two feet high, very variable.

Glaucus Willow. Bog Willow. *S. discolor*, Muhl.

Leaves, two to five inches long, one to nearly two inches wide, oblong or reverse egg-shape, pointed, unevenly toothed, teeth remote at the base, becoming finer and closer, and disappearing toward the apex. *Leaf-stem*, one half inch or more in length.

Found, common in damp grounds from Canada to North Carolina; seven to fifteen feet high.

Fig. 106.—Prairie Willow. *S. humilis*, Marsh.

Leaves, reverse lance-shape to oblong, pointed, or the lowest ones reverse egg-shape and obtuse; edge entire and often slightly rolled under, or "crinkly," very variable. *Leaf-stem*, distinct.

Found, common in dry fields; three to eight feet high.

Fig. 107.—Dwarf Gray Willow. *S. tristis*, Ait.

Leaves, one to two inches, crowded, very narrow reverse-lanceolate, tapering to a very short *leaf-stem*, edge entire and slightly wavy and somewhat rolled under. *Apex*, pointed or somewhat blunted, under surface often downy.

Found, common in dry ground, one to one and a half feet high, downy, with the leaves often clustered at the ends of the branches.

Fig. 108.—Silky Willow. Gray Willow. *S. sericea*, Marsh.

Leaves, two to three inches long, narrow lance-shape, taper-pointed, finely and evenly toothed, drying black, when young very silky.

Found, in low, wet ground, oftenest east of the Lakes; six to eight feet high.

Fig. 109.—Long-Stalked Green Osier. *S. petiolaris, Smith.*

Leaves, much as in the last, less liable to blacken in drying, and less silky when young.

Found, in low ground, oftenest west of the Lakes.

A bush four to fifteen feet high. The little twigs are used in basket-making.

S. argyrocárpa. *Anders.*

Leaves, one to two inches long, tapering evenly toward both ends, margin wavy-toothed, and slightly rolled back. *Leaf-stem*, short.

Found, in dense patches in high mountain ravines of New Hampshire and in Lower Canada and Labrador; one to two feet high.

Mountain Willow. *S. phylicifolia, L.*

Leaves, two to three inches long, egg-shape to lance-shape, remotely and finely toothed, very smooth above and below.

Found, in high ravines of the White Mountains, and on Mount Mansfield, Vermont; one to ten feet high.

Fig. 110.—Sage Willow. Hoary Willow. *S. cándida, Willd.*

Leaves, two to four inches or more in length, lance-shape or narrow lance-shape, mostly taper-pointed; edge entire or obscurely toothed at the apex, and rolled under; densely white-downy beneath.

Found, in cold, wet ground from New Jersey westward and northward.

A shrub two to six feet high, hoary, the new shoots white-woolly, the older shoots red.

Fig. 111.—Heart-Leaved Willow. *S. cordata, Muhl.*

Leaves, long lance-shape, sharp-toothed or nearly entire, not blackening in drying. *Base*, pointed to heart-shape. *Leaf-stem*, one third to one half inch long.

Found, very widely distributed in wet ground.

The most variable of American species.

Fig. 112.—S. balsamifera. *Barratt.*

Leaves, with base broadly rounded, and usually somewhat heart-shaped. *Leaf-stem*, long and slender.

Found, in wet land from Maine to Iowa, and northward, in clumps.

Fig 113.—S. myrtillòides. *L.*

Leaves, one to two inches long, reverse egg-shape to oblong, entire, blunt or slightly pointed, margin rolled under, smooth above and below.

Found, in cold swamps in New Jersey, and from New England to Iowa, and northward.

Bear-Berry Willow. *S. Ùva-ùrsi, Pursh.*

Leaves, sometimes elliptical and pointed, sometimes reverse egg-shape and blunt; less than one inch long, slightly toothed, strongly veined, smooth and shining above.

Found, abundantly over the high mountain summits of Northern New England and New York.

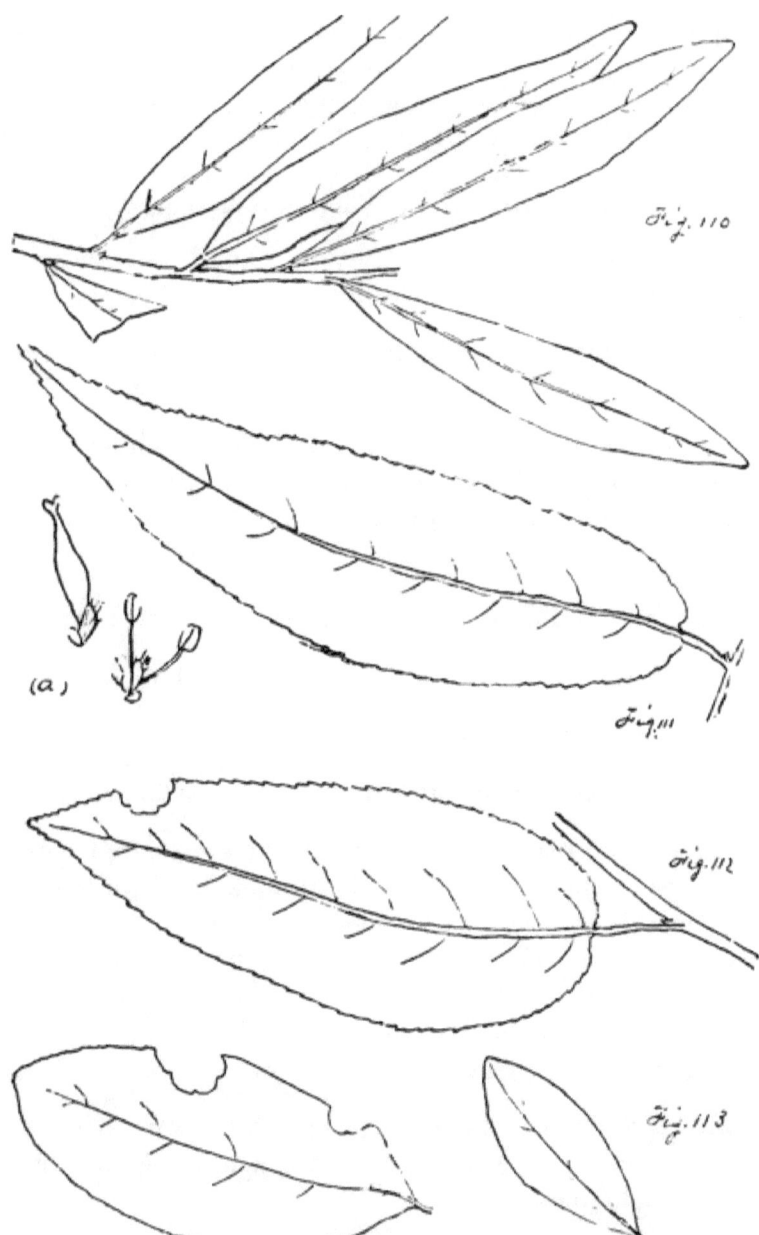

Fig. 110.—Sage Willow. (S. cándida, Willd.)
Fig. 111.—Heart-Leaved Willow. (S. cordàta, Muhl.)
(a) Staminate and pistillate flowers enlarged.
Fig. 112.—Pear-Leaved Willow. (S. balsamifera, Barratt.)
Fig. 113.—S. myrtillòides, L. (Two forms.)

Crow-Berry (Empetraceæ)

A low or prostrate shrub, spreading thickly over a surface from one to two feet in diameter.

Herb Willow. Arctic Willow. *S. herbàceæ, L.*

Leaves, about one inch long, nearly round. *Base*, heart-shaped, **toothed, veiny, smooth, and shining.**

Found, on the high summits of the mountains of New England and far northward.

The smallest of its family, with half underground creeping stems, and branches that seldom rise more than one or two inches above the surface.

33. Family EMPETRACEÆ. (Crow-Berry Fam.)

Genus CORÈMA, Don. (Broom Crow-Berry.)

From a Greek word meaning "broom."

Fig. 114.—Broom Crow-Berry. *C. Conràdii, Torr.*

Flowers, sometimes in the staminate and pistillate forms, and on different bushes; in terminal heads of ten to fifteen blossoms, each blossom in the axil of a scaly bract. *Corolla*, lacking. *Stamens*, three (rarely four), long and purple. *Style*, slender, mostly three-cleft. *Seed-case*, three- to four-celled, not adherent to the calyx. March, April.

Leaves, evergreen, one quarter inch long, very narrow, almost line-like, short, crowded, margins entire and rolled under.

Fruit, round, minute, with three (sometimes four or five) small nutlets; a drupe.

Crow-Berry (*Empetràceæ*)

Fig. 114.—Broom Crow-Berry. (C. Conrádii, Torr.)

Crow-Berry (Empetràceæ)

Found, in sandy barrens and in dry, rocky ground, mostly along the coast from New Jersey to Newfoundland, also in the Shawangunk Mountains of New York.

A much-branched evergreen heath-like shrub, six inches to two feet high.

Genus EMPETRUM, Tourn. (Black Crow-Berry.)

From two Greek words meaning "upon" and "a rock."

Black Crow-Berry. *E. nigrum,* L.

Flowers, reddish, inconspicuous in the angles of the upper leaves, with scaly bracts. *Corolla,* lacking. *Sepals,* three. *Stamens,* three. *Style,* one, very short, with six to nine rays. *Seed-case,* six- to nine-celled, not adherent to the calyx. May, June.

Leaves, about one quarter inch long, evergreen, crowded, lapping each other and covering the branches.

Fruit, round, black, a drupe with six to nine seed-like nutlets.

Found, in Mount Desert and along the coast of Maine, in the high mountains of New York and New England, and far northward.

A spreading and prostrate shrub with a stem one to four feet long.

CLASS SECOND
(Gymnospermæ)

34. Family CONÍFERÆ. (Pine Fam.)

Genus JUNÍPERUS, L. (Juniper.)

Fig. 115.—Common Juniper. *J. commùnis, L.*

Flowers, the staminate and pistillate forms usually on separate plants, in small clusters or cones at the sides of the branches. *Corolla* and *calyx*, lacking.

Leaves, evergreen, five twelfths to three quarters of an inch long, line-like, stiff, sharp, grooved and whitened above, green and ridged below; in clusters (whorls) of threes.

Fruit, bluish-black, one quarter of an inch or more in diameter, with one to three bony, wingless, egg-shaped seeds, ripening the second year from flowering; berry-like.

Found, common on dry land from New Jersey to Canada and Wisconsin.

An evergreen shrub, usually low and flat in large beds, with many spreading or drooping and rooting branches, yet sometimes rising six to eight feet in pyramidal form. The sweetish, turpentine-flavored berries are medicinal—diuretic and stimulating.

Pine (Coníferæ)

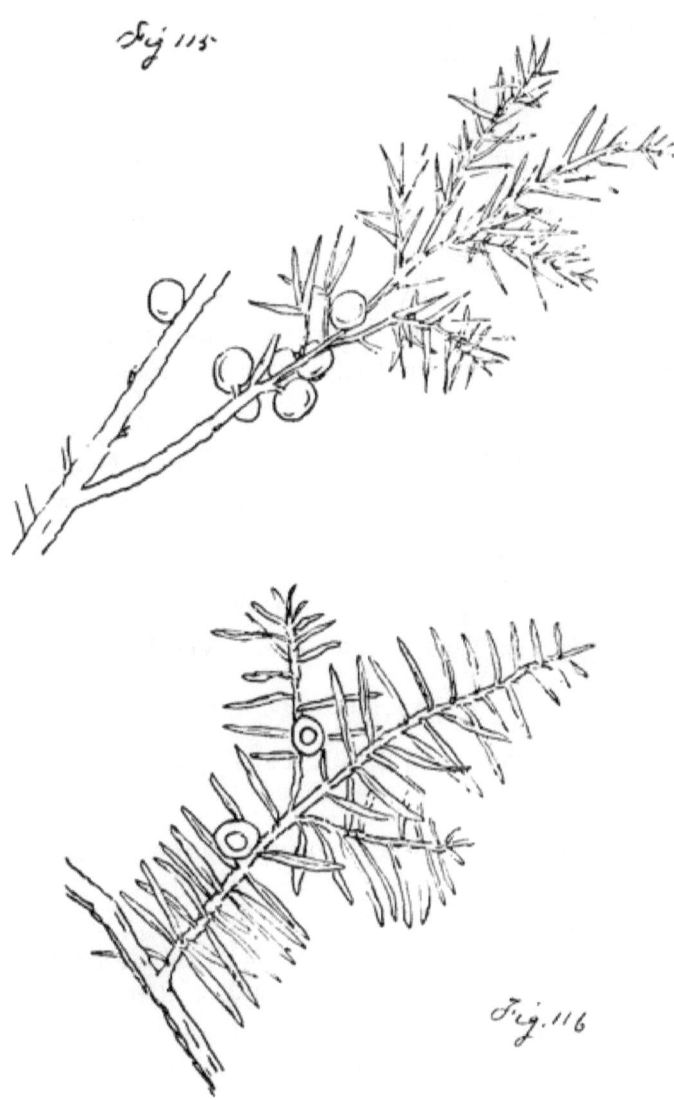

Fig. 115.—Common Juniper. (J. commùnis, L.)
Fig. 116.—American Yew. (T. Canadénsis, Willd.)

Var. alpìna, Gaud., is a prostrate form with leaves less spreading, and but one sixth to two sixths of an inch in length; found from Maine to Minnesota, and northward.

Prostrate Juniper.   *J. Sabìna, L., var. procùmbens, Pursh.*

This variety differs from the preceding chiefly in the following items:

Leaves, mostly opposite, a part awl-shaped and loose, the others scale-like and close to the branch and with a resinous gland on the back.

Fruit, on a short, curved stem.

Found, on rocky banks, borders of streams, etc., from New England to Northern Minnesota, and northward.

A prostrate or sometimes creeping shrub.

Genus Táxus.   (American Yew.)

From a Greek word meaning a "bow."

Fig. 116.—American Yew.   Dwarf Yew.   Ground Hemlock.
T. Canadénsis, Willd.

Flowers, at the sides of the branches, the staminate and pistillate forms usually on separate plants; the *staminate* form small and rounded, consisting merely of eight to ten stamens; the *pistillate*, solitary, consisting of an erect seed with a ring-like disk which expands and becomes cup-like, and finally pulpy and drupe-like, nearly covering the nut-like seed. May.

Leaves, evergreen, one half to two thirds of an inch long, line-like, stiff, sharp, flat, green above and below, arranged along the stem in two rows.

Fruit, red, about the size of a pea, slightly hollowed and open at the top, showing the black seed within; drupe-like. August, September.

Found, in shaded places, especially under other evergreens, from New Jersey westward and northward.

A low, straggling evergreen bush two to three feet high, often forming broad, flat clumps. Its wood is yellowish-brown, tough, and elastic. It was often used by the Indians in making their bows.

SHRUBS NOT ELSEWHERE NAMED.

Prùnus angustifòlia, Marsh.
Prùnus cuneàta, Raf.
Spirǽa Virginiana, Britton.
Rùbus negléctus, Peck.
Rùbus Millspàughii, Britton.
Rhododendron canéscens (Michx.), Porter.

" We see here a perpetuall Spring,
    A gallant flowering May,
Which month is painter of the world,
    As some great Clerks do say.
Rejoice in God . . .
    Who thus hath lent the strength,
And eke inspirde thee with such grace,
    To end this worke at length ;
And doubt not but herein thou hast
    Both pleasèd God and man :
Happie art thou in doing this,
    Happie when thou began."

"Thomas Thorney, to his learned friend and loving brother in Art. M. John Gerard."

(Quoted from Gerard's *Herball*, London, 1597.)

EXPLANATION OF TERMS, ETC.

EXPLANATION OF TERMS.

I.

Shrubs, as distinguished from trees, are those species which, as a rule, do not spring from the ground with a single branching trunk.

II.

THE FLOWER.

(1) The flower, when complete, is composed of *petals* Fig. a (1); *sepals*, Fig. a (2); *stamens*, Fig. b (1), with *filament*, Fig. b (2), and *anther*, Fig. b (3); *pistil*, Fig. b (4), with *seed-case*, Fig. b (5); *style*, Fig. b (6), and *stigma*, Fig. b (7).

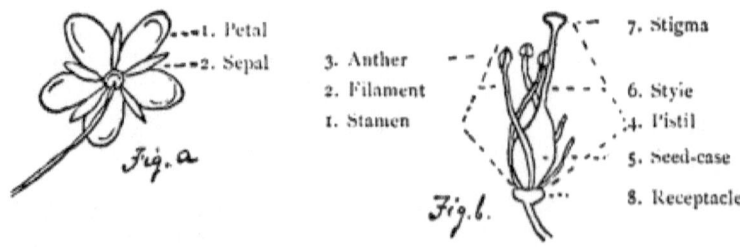

These parts are supported by the *receptacle*, Fig. b (8). The *corolla* (crown) is the circle of the petals; the *calyx* (cup) is the circle of the sepals.

(2) The flower is *pistillate*, when the pistil is present and the stamens are lacking; *staminate*, when the stamens are present and the pistil is lacking.

(3) The seed-case is *free*, when it is not attached along its sides to the calyx; *adherent*, when it is so attached.

(4) The flower is *terminal*, when it is at the end of a branch; *axillary*, when it springs from the base of the leaf-stem, *i. e.*, from the "axil" of the leaf.

III.

THE FRUIT.

The fruit consists of the ripened seeds and their wraps. For the different kinds see the Fruit Guide, page 29.

IV.

THE LEAF.

(1) A leaf is *simple*, when it is of one piece, Fig. *d*; *compound*, when there are two or more entirely distinct parts, called *leaflets* on the one leaf-stem, Fig. *e*.

A compound leaf is *feather-shaped*, when the leaflets are placed along the sides of the leaf-stem, Fig. *e*; *hand-shaped*, when all the leaflets radiate from the end of the leaf-stem, like fingers from the palm of the hand.*

(2) The leaf is *entire*, when its edge is an even line without indentations; *toothed*, when it is set with an indefinite number of sharp or blunt teeth; *lobed*, when the indentations are deep and of a definite number, Fig. *d*.

---

*NOTE 1.—Compound leaves may be once, twice, or three times compound.

NOTE 2.—The leaflets of a compound leaf can be distinguished from a simple leaf by the absence of leaf-buds from the base of their stems.

(3) The leaf is *needle-shaped*, or *line-shaped*, when it is very narrow, or sometimes scarcely more than a line, *e. g.*, Juniper and Yew; *lance-shape*, when it is much longer than wide, and gradually tapering to a point, *e. g.*, most Willows; *inversely lance-shape*, when gradually tapering down instead of up; *egg-shape*, when it is of the general shape of an egg, with the broadest part below the middle, but without regard to the form of the base and the apex, Fig. *c*; *inversely egg-shape*, when it is the shape of an

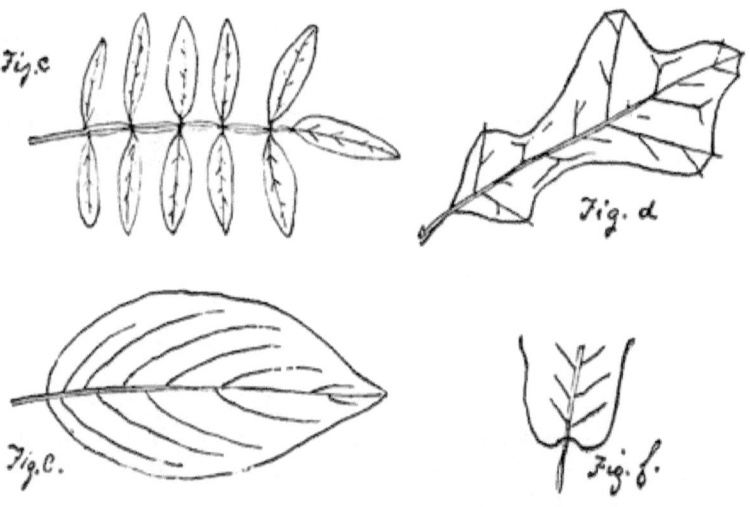

egg, but with the broadest part above the middle; *oval*, with the broadest part at the middle.

(4) The leaf at its apex may be *pointed*, *taper-pointed*, *bristle-pointed* (when it terminates in a bristle), Fig. *d*, *blunt* or *rounded*.

(5) The leaf at its base may be *squared*, *rounded*, *pointed*, *wedge-shape* (when it tapers to a point by straight lines), or *heart-shape*, Fig. *f*.

(6) The leaves as arranged upon the branch may be *alternate*, when they follow one another upon different

sides of the branch ; *opposite*, when they are in pairs and on opposite sides of the branches ; *indeterminate*, when they are closely crowded up and down the branches, *e. g.*, Hudsonia and Yew.

V.

(1) *Stipules* are appendages of the nature of a leaf, but of various forms, found in some plants in pairs at the base of the leaf-stems, *e. g.*, in the Rose.

(2) *Bracts* are small appendages of the nature of a leaf, but of various forms, found oftenest in connection with, or just below, the calyx, *e. g.*, in Leucóthoë.

(3) The *axil* of a vein or a leaf is the angle formed with another vein or with a branch.

GLOSSARY.

	PAGE		PAGE
Achènium or akene (see Fruit Guide, p. 29.)		Leaflet (distinguished from leaf)	237
Adherent	237	Legume (see Fruit Guide, p. 30)	
Alternate-leaved	238	Lobed	237
Angiospérmæ (plants whose seeds are covered)	19	Needle-shaped	238
		Opposite-leaved	239
Anther	239	Oval	238
Axil	237	Persistent (remaining in place after ripening)	
Axillary	237		
Berry (see Fruit Guide, p. 29)		Petal	19
Bract	239	Pistil	236
Bristle-pointed	238	Pistillate	236
Calyx	236	Pollen (the contents of the anther-cells)	
Compound leaf	236		
Corolla	236	Pome (see Fruit Guide, p. 29)	
Drupe (see Fruit Guide, p. 29)		Receptacle	236
Egg-shaped	238	Rounded	238
Entire-edged	237	Samara (see Fruit Guide, p. 29)	
Feather-shaped	237	Seed-case	236
Filament	236	Sepal	236
Follicle (see Fruit Guide, p. 29)		Shrub (distinguished from tree)	236
Free	237	Simple leaf	237
Fruit	237	Squared	238
Gymnospérmæ (plants whose seeds are naked)	24	Stamen	236
		Staminate	236
Hand-shaped	237	Stigma	236
Heart-shaped	238	Style	236
Indeterminate-leaved	239	Taper-pointed	238
Inverse egg- or lance-shaped	238	Toothed-edge	237
Lance-shaped	238	Twice compound	237
Leaflet	237	Wedge-shaped	238

SHRUBS WORTHY OF CULTIVATION.

	PAGE		PAGE
Barberry	38	Hydrangea	111
St.-John's-worts	44	Witch-Hazel	118
Prickly Ash (for Hedges)	47	Angelica Tree	122
Hop Tree	50	Dogwoods (Cornels)	126
Inkberry	54	Viburnums	134
Burning-Bush	58	Snowberry	144
Buckthorn (for Hedges)	62	Tartarian Honeysuckle	149
New Jersey Tea	64	Leucöthoë	149
Bladder-Nut	68	Groundsel Tree	154
Sumachs	70	Stagger-Bush	168
Meadow-Sweet	86	Kalmias	176
Steeple-Bush	88	Rhododendrons	180
Nine-Bark	88	Fringe-Tree	190
Roses	88	Privet	190
Thorns (Cratægus)	104	Shepherdia	198
Sweet-scented Shrub	110		

INDEX OF SHRUBS.

The names of families are given in CAPITALS, of genera in SMALL CAPITALS, of species and varieties in "roman type," and synonyms in *italics*. The names of introduced species are enclosed by brackets.

A	PAGE
ACER spicàtum	66
Alder, *Black*	52
Green	209
Hoary	210
Mountain	209
Smooth	210
Speckled	210
White	188
Wild	210
Allspice, Carolina	110
Wild	110
ÀLNUS incàna	210
serrulàta	210
víridis	209
AMELÀNCHIER Canadénsis	108
var. alnifòlia	110
var. oblongifòlia	110
var. oligocárpa	110
spicàta	110
AMÓRPHA canéscens	78
fructicòsa	78
ANACARDIÀCEÆ	70
ANDRÓMEDA ligustrìna	160
Mariàna	165
polifòlia	166
Andromeda, Marsh	166
Privet	160
Angelica Tree	122
ANONÀCEÆ	38
ARALIÀCEÆ	122
ARÀLIA spinòsa	122
Arrow-wood	133
Arrow-wood, Downy	140

	PAGE
Arrow-wood, *Maple-leaved*	135
ÀSCYRUM Crux Àndreæ	45
stans	44
Ash, Northern Prickly	47
ASÍMINA trilòba	38
Azalea, Clammy	179
Flame-colored	182
Purple	180
Smooth	180

B

	PAGE
BÁCCHARIS halimifòlia	154
Barberry	38
BARBERRY	38
Bayberry	202
Bay, Rose	182
Sweet	36
Beach Plum	82
Bear Oak	213
Beech, *Blue*	214
Water	214
Benjamin-bush	194
BERBERIDÀCEÆ	38
BÉRBERIS [vulgàris]	38
BÉTULA glandulòsa	208
papyrífera var. minor	208
pùmila	208
Bilberry, Bog	164
Birch, Low	208
Black Alder	52
Blackberry, High	94
Sand	94

Index of Shrubs

	PAGE		PAGE
Blackcap	92	COMPOSITE	154
Black Thorn	84	CONÍFERÆ	230
Bladder-Nut, American	68	Coral-berry	146
Blueberry, Common Low	162	CORÈMA Conrádii	226
Common High	163	CORNÀCEÆ	124
Dwarf	162	Cornel, Alternate-leaved	127
Low	163	Long-leaved	126
Swamp	163	Panicled	127
Blue Tangle	159	Round-leaved	124
BUCKTHORN	61	Silky	126
Buckthorn, Alder-leaved	62	Cornel	126
Carolina	62	CÓRNUS alternifòlia	127
[Common]	62	asperifòlia	126
Lance-leaved	61	candidíssima	127
Buffalo-Nut	200	circinàta	124
Burning-Bush	58	paniculàta	127
Bush Honeysuckle	150	sericea	126
Button-Bush	152	stolonífera	126
		CÓRYLUS Americàna	212
C		rostràta	214
		Cranberry, Bush	134
Calico-Bush	174	High	134
CALYCANTHÀCEÆ	110	Tree	134
CALYCANTHUS	110	CRATÆGUS coccínea	104
CALYCÁNTHUS flóridus	111	var. macrácantha	104
lævigatus	110	var. móllis	104
nànus	110	crus-gálli	106
CAPRIFOLIÀCEÆ	130	[oxyacántha]	108
Carolina Allspice	110	parvifòlia	108
CÁRPINUS Carolina	214	tomentòsa	106
Cassandra	171	unifòra	108
CASSÁNDRA calyculàta	171	Crow-berry, Black	228
CASTÀNEA pùmila	218	Broom	226
CEANÒTHUS Americànus	64	CROW-BERRY	226
ovàtus	64	CROWFOOT	34
Ceanothus, Narrow-leaved	64	CUPULÍFERÆ	206
CELASTRÀCEÆ	58	Currant, Indian	146
CEPHALÁNTHUS occidentàlis	152	Currant, Wild Black	118
Cherry, Choke	84	Wild Red	118
Chestnut, Dwarf	218	Custard-Apple	38
Chinquapin	218		
CHIONÁNTHUS Virginica	190	D	
Chokeberry	100		
Choke-Cherry	84	Dangleberry	159
CISTÀCEÆ	42	Daphne	198
CLÉTHRA alnifòlia	188	DAPHNE	196
Cockspur Thorn	106	DÁPHNE Mezéreum	198
COMPÓSITÆ	154	Deerberry	160

Index of Shrubs

	PAGE
Devil's Walking-Stick . .	
DIERVÍLLA trífida . .	122
DÍRCA palústris . . .	150
Dockmackie . . .	196
Dogberry . . .	138
DOGWOOD . . .	102
Dogwood . . .	124
Alternate-leaved	127
Long-leaved .	126
Panicled .	127
Poison .	74
Round-leaved	124
Silky .	126
Dutch *Myrtle* .	204

E

Eglantine . .	100
ELÆAGNÀCEÆ	198
Elder, Common .	130
Poison .	74
Red-berried	132
EMPETRÀCEÆ	226
ÉMPETRUM nigrum	228
ERICÀCEÆ . .	155
EUÓNYMUS Americànus	60
atropurpùreus .	58

F

False Indigo .	78
Fern, Sweet . .	205
Fever-Bush . .	194
Fly Bracted . .	149
Honeysuckle .	146
Mountain .	148
Swamp . .	148
Fringe-Tree . .	190

G

Gale, Sweet . . .	204
GAYLUSSÀCIA brachýcera	159
dumòsa .	158
frondòsa .	159
resinòsa .	160
GINSENG . . .	124
Gooseberry, Common Wild .	114
Missouri .	116
Prickly .	114

	PAGE
Gooseberry, Round-leaved	116
Swamp	116
Ground Hemlock .	232
Groundsel Tree	154
Guelder Rose	136

H

HAMAMELÍDEÆ	118
Hamamèlis Virgínica	118
Hardhack .	88
Haw, Black .	142
Red .	104
[Hawthorn, English]	108
Hazel-Nut, Beaked	214
Wild .	212
HEATH . .	155
Hemlock, Ground .	232
Hercules Club .	122
Highwater Shrub	154
Hobble-Bush .	134
HOLLY . .	50
Holly, Mountain .	56
HONEYSUCKLE	130
Honeysuckle-Bush	150
Fly . .	146
Tartarian	149
White Swamp .	179
Hop Tree .	50
Hornbeam . .	214
Huckleberry, Box	159
Common Black	156
Dwarf	158
Squaw	160
Hudsonia . .	42
HUDSÒNIA ericòides	44
tomentòsa .	42
HYDRÁNGEA arborescens	111
Hydrangea, Wild	111
HYPERICÀCEÆ .	44
HYPÉRICUM densiflòrum	46
Kalmiànum	47
prolíficum	46

I

ÍLEX glàbra .	54
lævigàta	54
móllis .	52

Index of Shrubs

	PAGE		PAGE
Ílex montàna	52	[Ligústrum vulgàre]	190
monticola	52	Líndera Benzoin	194
verticillàta	52	Lonicèra cerùlea	148
Ilex, Soft	52	ciliàta	146
ILICÍNEÆ	50	involucràta	149
Indian Currant	146	oblongifòlia	148
Indigo False	78	Tartárica	149
Inkberry	54	Loranthàceæ	199
Ironwood	214		
Itea	112	**M**	
Iteà Virginica	112	MADDER	152
Iva frutéscens	154	MAGNOLIÀCEÆ	36
Ivy, Poison	76	MAGNOLIA	36
		Magnòlia, *glauca*	36
J		Virginiàna	36
June-Berry	108	*Magnolia, Small*	36
Juniper, Common	230	Maple, Mountain	66
Prostrate	232	Marsh Elder	154
JUNÍPERUS commùnis	230	*May Cherry*	108
var. Alpìna	232	Meadow-Sweet	86
Sabìna var. procumbens	232	MENZIÈSIA glabélla	178
		globulàris	178
K		Mezereum	198
KÁLMIA angustifòlia	176	MISTLETOE	199
glauca	176	Mistletoe, American	199
latifòlia	174	*Moosewood*	196
Kinnikinnik	126	*Mountain Maple*	66
		MYRÌCA asplenifòlia	205
L		cerífera	202
Labrador Tea	186	Gàle	204
Lambkill	176	MYRICÀCEÆ	202
Lapland, Rose Bay	185		
LAURÀCEÆ	194	**N**	
LAUREL	194	NEMOPÁNTHES *fasciculàris*	56
Laurel, *Great*	182	mucronàta	56
Mountain	174	New Jersey Tea	64
Pale	176	Nine-Bark	88
Sheep	176		
Swamp	36	**O**	
Lead-Plant	78	OAK	206
Leather-Leaf	171	Oak, Bear	218
Leatherwood	196	Dwarf Chestnut	216
LÈDUM latifòlium	186	Poison	76
[palùstre]	186	*Scrub* (Q. illicifòlia)	218
LEGUMINÒSÆ	78	*Scrub* (Q. M. var. hùmilis)	216
Leucothoë	169	*Old Man's Beard*	190
LEUCÓTHOË racemòsa	169	OLEÀCEÆ	190

Index of Shrubs 247

	PAGE		PAGE
OLEASTER	198	Red Osier	126
Oil-nut	200	Red-root	64
OLIVE	190	RHAMNÀCEÆ	61
Osier, Long-stalked	223	RHAMNUS alnifòlia	62
		Caroliniàna	62
P		[cathártica]	62
Papaw	38	lanceolàta	61
PAPAW	38	Rhododendron	182
Pepper-Bush, Sweet	188	RHODODÉNDRON arboréscens	180
PHORADÉNDRON flavéscens	199	calendulàceum	182
PHYSOCÀRPUS opulifòlius	88	Canadénse	184
PINE	230	canéscens	233
Pinxter-flower	180	Lappónicum	185
Plum, Beach	82	máximum	182
Canada	81	nudiflòrum	180
Horse	81	var. polyándra	182
Wild	81	Rhodòra	184
Poison Ivy	76	viscòsum	179
Oak	76	var. glaucum	180
Sumach	74	var. nítidum	180
Prickly Ash, Northern	47	Rhodora	
[Privet]	190	RHUS aromática	76
PRÙNUS Alleghaniénsis	82	Canadénsis	76
Americàna	81	copallìna	73
angustifòlius	233	glabra	70
cuneàta	233	radicans	76
marítima	82	toxicodéndron	76
pùmila	81	typìna	72
[spinòsa]	84	venenàta	74
Virginiàna	84	Vérnix	74
PTÈLEA trifoliàta	50	RIBES Cynósbati	114
PULSE	78	flòridum	118
PYRULÀRIA pùbera	200	grácile	116
PŸRUS arbutifòlia	100	lacústre	116
" var. melanocárpa	102	oxycanthòìdes	114
nigra	102	rotundifòlium	116
		rubrum, var. subglandu-	
Q		lòsum	118
QUÉRCUS ilicifòlia	218	ROCK-ROSE	42
Muhlenbérgii, Eng., var.		RÒSA blánda	98
hùmilis, Britton	216	Carolìna	98
		[rubiginòsa]	100
R		hùmilis	97
RANUNCULÀCEÆ	34	lùcida	97
Raspberry, Black	92	nítida	98
Purple-flowering	90	ROSÀCEÆ	80
Wild Red	92	Rose Bay	182
Red Haw	104		

Index of Shrubs

	PAGE		PAGE
Rose, Bland	98	Scrub Oaks (see Oak)	216
Carolina	98	Service Tree	108
Low	97	Shad-Bush	108
Shining	97	Sheep-Laurel	176
Swamp	98	SHEPHÉRDIA Canadénsis	198
Wild	98	Shrub Yellow-Root	34
ROSE	80	Shrubby Trefoil	50
Rosemary	166	[Sloe (P. spinosa)]	84
RUBIÀCEÆ	152	Sloe (V. prunifolium)	142
Rubus cuneifólius	94	Smooth Winterberry	54
negléctus	233	Snowberry	144
Millspáughii	233	Snowball	136
occidentális	92	SOAPBERRY	66
odorátus	90	Spice-Bush	194
strigósus	92	Spindle-Tree	58
villósus	94	SPIRÆA corymbòsa	86
var. frondòsus	94	salicifòlia	86
RUE	47	tomentòsa	88
RUTACEÆ	47	Virginiàna	233
		Spiræa, Birch-leaved	86
S		Spoonwood	174
		Squaw Huckleberry	160
Saint Andrew's Cross	45	STAFF-TREE	58
ST.-JOHN'S-WORT	44	Stag-Bush	142
Saint-John's-wort, Shrubby Kalms	44	Stagger-Bush	168
Saint-Peter's-wort	44	STAPHYLÈA trifolia	68
SALICÀCEÆ	220	Steeple-Bush	88
SALIX argyrocárpa	223	Strawberry-Bush	60
balsamifera	224	Sumach, Dwarf	73
cándida	223	Mountain	73
cordàta	224	Smooth	70
discolor	222	Stag-horn	72
herbàceæ	226	Sweet	76
húmilis	222	Poison	74
longifòlia	220	SUMACH	70
myrtillòides	224	Swamp Laurel	36
petiolàris	223	Swamp Pink	179
phylicifòlia	223	Sweet-Bay	36
sericea	222	Sweet-Brier	100
tristis	222	Sweet-Fern	205
Uva-úrsi	224	Sweet-Gale	204
SAMBÚCUS Canadénsis	130	SWEET-GALE	202
racemòsa	132	Sweet-scented Shrub	110
SANTALÀCEÆ	200	SYMPHORICÁRPOS occidentàlis	144
SANDAL-WOOD	200	orbiculàris	146
SAPINDÀCEÆ	66	racemòsus	144
SAXIFRAGÀCEÆ	111	var. pauciflòrus	144
SAXIFRAGE	111	vulgàris	146

Index of Shrubs

T

	PAGE
Tartarian Honeysuckle	149
Taxus Canadénsis	232
Tea, Labrador	186
New Jersey	64
Thimbleberry	92
[Thorn, Black (P. spinósa)]	84
Thorn, Black (C. tomentósa)	106
Cockspur	106
Dwarf	108
Pear	106
Scarlet-fruited	104
White	104
THYMELEÀCEÆ	196
Toothache Tree	47
Trefoil, Shrubby	50

V

	PAGE
Vaccínium Canadénse	162
cæspitósum	164
var. cuneifólium	164
corymbósum	163
var. atrocócum	163
myrtillóides	164
ovalifólium	164
Pennsylvánicum	162
var. angustifólium	162
var. nigrum	162
staminèum	160
uliginósum	164
vacillans	163
Vibúrnum acerifólium	138
cassinóides	142
dentátum	138
lantanóides	134
mólle	140
núdum	140
ópulus	134
paucifólium	136

	PAGE
Vibúrnum prunifólium	142
pubéscens	140
Viburnum, Few-flowered	136
Soft	140

W

	PAGE
Waahoo	58
Wax Myrtle	202
Wayfaring Tree, American	134
Willow, Arctic	226
Bear-Berry	224
Bog	222
Dwarf Gray	222
Glaucus	222
Gray	222
Heart-leaved	224
Herb	226
Hoary	223
Long-leaved	220
Mountain	223
Prairie	222
Sage	223
Silky	222
WILLOW	220
Winterberry	52
Smooth	54
Witch Hazel	118
WITCH HAZEL	118
Withe-rod (V. cassinóides)	142
(V. núdum)	140
Wolf-Berry	144

X

	PAGE
XANTHORHÌZA apifólia	34
XANTHÓXYLUM Americànum	47

Y

	PAGE
Yellow-Root, Shrub	34
Yew, American	232
Yew, Dwarf	232

www.ingramcontent.com/pod-product-compliance
Lightning Source LLC
Chambersburg PA
CBHW020802230426
43666CB00007B/807